CULTIVATING LEADERS FROM WITHIN

A GUIDE TO "GROWING LEADERSHIP"

Raimi-Akinleye Abiodun

Author's Tranquility Press
ATLANTA, GEORGIA

Copyright © 2024 by Raimi-Akinleye Abiodun

All rights reserved. No part of this publication may be reproduced, distributed or transmitted in any form or by any means, including photocopying, recording, or other electronic or mechanical methods, without the prior written permission of the publisher, except in the case of brief quotations embodied in critical reviews and certain other noncommercial uses permitted by copyright law. For permission requests, write to the publisher, addressed "Attention: Permissions Coordinator," at the address below.

Raimi-Akinleye Abiodun /Author's Tranquility Press
3900 N Commerce Dr. Suite 300 #1255
Atlanta, GA 30344, USA
www.authorstranquilitypress.com

Ordering Information:
Quantity sales. Special discounts are available on quantity purchases by corporations, associations, and others. For details, contact the "Special Sales Department" at the address above.

Cultivating Leaders from Within: A Guide to "Growing Leadership" / Raimi-Akinleye Abiodun
Hardback: 978-1-964810-63-8
Paperback: 978-1-964810-34-8
eBook: 978-1-964810-35-5

Contents

Acknowledgments 1
About the Author 3
Introduction 4
Part 1 ....
   Chapter 1 Leadership Styles 9
   Chapter 2 Leadership Development 25
   Chapter 3 Leadership Awareness 35
   Chapter 4 People First, Not Policy 43
   Chapter 5 Learn to Listen and Communicate 55
   Chapter 6 Be Inclusive 67
   Chapter 7 Support and Create a Learning Culture 81
Part 2 ....
   Chapter 8 Support Creativity 95
   Chapter 9 Be a Focused Change Agent 104
   Chapter 10 The Power of a Moral and Ethical Leader 112
   Chapter 11 Be an Engaging Leader 118
   Chapter 12 Building Strategic Direction 124
   Chapter 13 Foster an Environment of Thinkers 133
   Conclusion 138
   Bibliography 139
End Notes 143

I am dedicating this book to those black and other minority professionals who are judged by their color and not by the contents of their brains. I want you to know that God has your back, so fear not and believe. Your reward and harvest are coming; you just need to remain faithful and focused, and know that God is in control.

Your courage to stand and face all the tribulations and injustices is setting examples for those who are looking at you as their role model. Don't give up. God is with you; you just need to be hopeful in Him.

I would also like to dedicate this book to minority business professionals whose advancement is often hindered by their race instead of propelled by their qualifications and experience.

And let us not be weary in well doing: for in due season we shall reap, if we faint not. As we have therefore opportunity, let us do well unto all men, especially unto them who are of the household of faith. —Galatians 6:9–10

Acknowledgments

Looking back at my life professionally and personally, I recognize the significant things that people have contributed to my growth and development. I thank my parents for their vision, encouragement, and prayers when they were here with me and most importantly now that they are with our Maker and Savior.

It's a privilege to thank those who have contributed positively to my development. My brother, Sam Babatunde, I want you to know that I wholeheartedly appreciate all that you have done for me and my family. I remember those days when you used to force and encourage me to read and be a good student by facing my academic studies; for all this I say thank you.

I have been fortunate to have many excellent and dedicated mentors during my journey as a person and as a leader. As I stated above, my parents and brother were the first people who taught me the power of honesty, integrity, and steadfastness. The power of prayer and faith in the Lord and the lesson to only trust in God and not in any human being were all passed down to me by them.

I would like to thank the following people who have served as my mentors during the course of my professional journey: Mrs. Shelly Morgan, my executive vice president when I was new to management at Prince George's Hospital, introduced me to what was needed for me to be a good nurse manager. She asked me to be open, honest, and loyal to my staff and more importantly to the organization.

I would like to extend my thanks to Mr. Denis Swan and Mrs. Elizabeth Henry, who were president and vice president, respectively, when I was unit manager at Sparrow Health care System. They taught me the power of teamwork and system thinking. They taught me to always look at the forest and not the tree whenever I am ready to make decision that will impact my staff and the organization as a whole.

Another person to thank is Linda Rankin, who helped me fine-tune my leadership skills and showed me the importance of developing the people I am leading and know how to tap into their hidden potentials for the good of the organization.

It's my pleasure to also thank Alicia Coe and Michael Hampton for introducing me to the VA health care system. I learned from them the power of safety culture and what needs to be done when creating an environment that enhances and promotes the psychological safety of employees. Thanks to Mr. Daniel Handee, my previous medical director and current mentor, for his leadership and encouragement.

For what all these people have done to contribute to my growth and development, I am pleased and honored to have come across them; they have helped me with my career and leadership development. Your support and words of encouragement have contributed to who I am now and what I am hoping and dreaming to be.

About the Author

Abiodun Raimi was born and raised in Nigeria, where he had his early education before coming to the United States. He attended Duquesne University in Pittsburgh and earned his bachelor's degree in nursing. He later attended the University of Maryland for graduate education and University of Phoenix for his doctorate. He holds a doctoral degree in management with a concentration in leadership and organizational development. His graduate degree is in health care administration.

During his professional career, he has worked as a clinical associate, working hand in hand with other nurses to provide and promote quality health care delivery to patients. He has worked as assistant head nurse, nurse manager, and director of nursing operations and finance before he joined the Veteran Health Administration. Other roles came when he became associate chief nurse for acute, ambulatory, and long-term care services. All these roles exposed him to different health care needs, wants, and challenges of people in general.

He often cites as one of his greatest accomplishments the opportunity to be the author of two books and co-author of another. These books concentrate on management and management principles.

When not working in the hospital or office, he is the proud owner of a small management consulting firm, as well as owner and president of First Basic School in Delaware, where he conducts nursing reviews.

Introduction

I have come to believe that every organization aiming to be the best has to have a dynamic person at the top who will help with its direction. This future has to be based on vision, missions, and principles. People are looking for a great company to be part of, a place that could help develop and maintain a lasting relationship with people within and outside the organization. But most of these people often don't know if the organization's culture will allow them to achieve some of these goals.

This is true today, as we've seen what has happened to people in various organizations. Some were not able to achieve any of their career goals because of the type of culture and working environment that was directly or indirectly created. Some organizations have strict hierarchical cultures where one cannot advance without the support and recommendation of one's supervisors or the vacancy of a higher position. Some organizations have cultures where there is little or no investment in cross training, and staff are expected to follow procedures without adding input. To navigate current opportunities, not only is the culture vital to the growth and development of each employee, it's important that the organization have a leader at the top who could help with the vision, mission, and goals of the organization and its employees.

Every organization has to know that today's businesses are in constant flux, customers are global and ever-changing, and most importantly, products' life cycles are shorter than they used to be. These constant changes require a leader who is strong, forward-thinking, and able to understand some of the human dynamics that could help create a better and more productive organization.

The question that is being asked by various organizations is how they can manage in the current possibilities in today's environment. I have examined many successful organizations, like General Electric Corporation, Microsoft, and Apple. I have also read many reviewed articles on organizations and their leadership to learn some of the principles that have contributed to their successes.[1][2]

I also wanted to know why these organizations are succeeding despite all odds. I wanted to know some of the things that are attracting people to them, to learn secrets that have contributed to their long-lasting gains, and finally, to discover what others can learn from them. I concluded that these organizations are doing well because of the people at the top of their hierarchies. I concluded that there are some basic organizational and leadership skills that every leader must have, most importantly for every new leader who is growing and developing, and it's these basic leadership skills that will help seasoned and new leaders navigate the ups and downs that often occur in business. More importantly, these basic skills will help leaders successfully manage their organizations through the ups and downs to ensure their organization's sustainability and future success. These are basic leadership skills, which if used and applied effectively, can help lay a strong and lasting foundation for every leader and allow the leader to be successful and effective.

Cultivating Leadership from Within will help in the analysis and explanation of these basic leadership skills. The book will help you discover your own leadership style and skills that could help move you into the great leader column. The book will also provide you with reasons why good leadership skills and principles are the key factors for a successful organization and provide guidelines on human relation, human innovation, and human thinking, which are the new possibilities in today's organizations.

As it relates to human relations, *Cultivating Leadership from Within* describes the power of respect, communication, listening, and feedback and explains how a powerful and meaningful working relationship can help an organization achieve greatness. The new educated workers who are just joining the workforce are looking for leaders who can communicate with and listen to them; these new workers want to know the leaders are dependable partners. Building solid relationships could be the determining factor in propelling the organization to the next level of greatness.

Cultivating Leaders from Within looks at the human innovation and how workers who take risks are better than those who avoid risk. Innovation can only happen when employees are free to think, to communicate with each other and share knowledge, and above all, dialogue on critical issues that affect the organization. Rather than focusing energy on how to maintain competitive edge, it will be necessary for future leaders to begin to look at innovation and investing in new business models. Employees must begin to learn how to dive into the new age and see innovation as the new process for continuous evolution. The new environment must encourage knowledge sharing amongst members. These new workers prefer a spiral structure for knowledge transfer within the organization. Knowledge workers are innovators; they are creators, which mean the need for leaders to develop good sense of understanding of their employees, themselves, and their surroundings is on the increase and must be embraced by leaders at all level of the organization.

Innovation needs an effective and encouraging culture, one that incentivizes employees to start building diverse and inclusive teams. For innovation to work and be meaningful, leaders must be coaches and developers. They must be facilitators and teachers, recognizing that employees are their most valuable resources.

A new possibility could help an organization achieve its goals of moving from being a good company to a great one. Employees must see themselves as part of the team and that their contributions are meaningful and valued. This book looks at factors that could be implemented to help improve participation, engagement, and overall satisfaction. *Cultivating Leaders from Within* examines the impact of caring and supportive leaders on employees' thinking and performance. A leader who is caring, compassionate, and understanding will be able to initiate positive employee thinking. Leaders' flexibility and adaptability is crucial to the development of an organization that has more creative and innovative workers, because they are the ones who are going to help with the strategy implementation and sustainability. The psychological safety of the employees shall be enhanced when they know they are free to contribute meaningfully in the decision-making processes of the organization.

Cultivating Leadership from Within includes several methods that are used to explain each point and model. I strongly believe the explanations will allow for better understanding of each concept. I also know that applying any of the concepts will require a radical change by leaders, who will need to adopt some of these principles with no hesitation or doubt. Having been part of various periods of change in the organizations where I have worked, I can tell you that making changes takes courage and persistence. The practices that are explained in this book allow for flexibility, and more importantly, they allow you to manage your organization more effectively and efficiently. They allow you to be more oriented to staff needs and concerns and to promote a working environment that enhances innovation, human relations, and human thinking that could be used toward growth and development of the organization.

Part 1

Human Relations

Chapter 1
Leadership Styles

We know from experience that there is a big difference between the old management philosophy of yesterday—of parenting, organizing, leading, instructing, and evaluating—to that of today's PARTNER model: producing, assessing, responsibility, teamwork, negotiating with emotional intelligence, and reflection. This PARTNER concept is what the current X and Y generations are looking for in their working environments. They will be flexible and respect your leadership if you show them that you are caring and trusting. You should know that employees follow their leaders not because they are perfect or error free but because they exhibit behaviors that show their followers that they care. They demonstrate ultimate sincerity and openness in their daily activities and interactions. This means people know who they are and what their missions and visions are for their organizations. They help contribute to individual goals in addition to focusing on organizational goals. They know that leadership is more than the title and the power the position commands. They feel that one of the leader's responsibilities is being respectful of the people they lead. Success comes when people think you are a leader who keeps his or her words, that you do what you say you will and you model your behavior accordingly. When you are consistent in your behavior and your followers are able to see that this behavior is in alignment with the organization's values, beliefs, and norms, the probability of being a successful leader greatly increases.

One of the goals of this book is to help new as well as seasoned leaders discover their own styles and to see the relationship between leadership styles and employee effectiveness. It's true that some leaders are effective and successful and others are less so. Most of the authors and students of leadership have attributed this to leadership styles and how they are applied by different leaders. To be able to do this successfully, this chapter will examine some common styles associated with highly rated leaders of our time. The book will look at individual styles and how they helped their organizations.

Individual characteristics reflect leadership styles. Such characteristics as personality traits, abilities, and experience can help predict leadership effectiveness and leader-employee relationships. Organizations seek leaders who are not only intelligent but have the ability to instill needed values and discipline in their followers as well as themselves.

There are basic skills that any leader must have to be successful, which range from respect, ability to listen, communication, understanding, appreciation, and flexibility. We will later examine some of these skills.

In his book on Martin Luther King Jr., Donald T. Phillips (2000) wrote, "Leadership is leaders acting—as well as caring, inspiring, and persuading others to act—for certain shared goals that represent the values—the wants and needs, the aspirations and expectations—of themselves and the people they represent."

If we look objectively, we will see that leadership remains one of the most influential factors on employee performance and behavior. How an employee sees the organization and his or her role will depend on the type of leader who is instructing this employee. The growth of the organization rests on the type of leaders and their leadership styles. We know leader behaviors that influence productivity and performance will have the same positive effects on employees' behaviors and performance as well. The same is true if the leader's behavior is negative and less attractive for others to emulate, the possibility of having negative influence on employees is very high. It's important to note that for any increase in productivity to happen in any organization, employees of the organization must have high level of trust on their leaders. Growing leaders should always look for skills that will help with skills improvement and those skills that will help in the creation of a positive working culture.

In a more practical sense, a leader could be seen as a catalyst for organizational, group, and individual greatness, which provides another meaning to leadership by looking at leadership behaviors that could be used to motivate, educate, and encourage employees to have a positive look at the organization and its environment.

A close examination of leadership functions in the organization shows that there are some behaviors that could help enhance and uphold the values and vision of the organization when the leaders positively demonstrate these behaviors.

There are many different leadership styles. This book will examine the following types:

- directive leadership
- empowering leadership
- servant leadership
- transformational leadership
- authoritarian or autocratic leadership
- democratic leadership

Each one has unique characteristics and needs, and they all have the tendency to influence employee behavior and performance. The ultimate aim of the organization is to help itself by using leadership styles that could lead to better productivity and greater employee satisfaction and performance. Your goal is to help not only the organization but the employees in the achievement of organizational goals and objectives. It's an expectation that employees will grow professionally and personally under your leadership. How can you facilitate this? By demonstrating behaviors that are positive and inspiring; by cultivating an attitude of caring and listening; by being able to communicate effectively to employees both the organizational and departmental visions and missions; by being a willing team player; and by being able to look at issues from a larger context and not as isolated occurrences. In other words, this means as a leader you're able to look at the forest and not only the tree.

All these behaviors would be evidenced by how a leader understands human nature and reacts to diversity of expressions, thoughts, and cultures. Your effectiveness will also depend on your expression of ethical and moral behaviors, which are essential for the creation of a performing culture in the organization.

As we examine each of these leadership styles, you will see that some if not all demonstrate these skills and principles, and their influence could be seen in the growth level of the organization and its employees.

Effective leadership can be financially beneficial to an organization. It could help reduce employee turnover and improve employee and customer satisfaction and loyalty. It could lead to better management and productivity. The organization wants you to be inspirational to your employees, because inspirational leaders tend to be passionate and enthusiastic. In general terms, most inspirational leaders help others discover for themselves those things that contribute to their happiness.

Leadership directly impacts employees' satisfaction and level of engagement. In a recent study by Joseph Warren L. Perez (2014), which examined the impact of nurse managers' leadership styles, it was discovered that "Nursing retention presents many challenges and can be affected by many variables, including leadership styles" (Force 2005).

Your leadership style can contribute to the growth of the organization and serve as a catalyst for the development of human capital within the organization. A leadership style that enhances trust between employees and leaders could help in the development of the individual and the organization.

To help identify your leadership style, a brief explanation of each will be discussed below.

Servant Leadership

Servant leadership is a highly debated concept in organizations. It was introduced in 1970 by Robert K. Greenleaf in "The Servant as Leader,"

Greenleaf stated,

> The servant-leader is servant first.... It begins with the natural feeling that one wants to serve, to serve first. Then conscious choice brings one to aspire to lead. That person is sharply different from one who is leader first; perhaps because of the need to assuage an unusual power drive or to acquire material possessions. The leader-first and the servant-first are two extreme types. Between them there are shadings and blends that are part of the infinite variety of human nature.

This leadership style is about growing employees into their potential and is based on a working relationship between the leader and the employee. A servant leader believes in the human relations style of management and its advantages for the organization. A servant leader makes sure employees' needs are met and exceeded; the leader knows the solution does not reside in him alone; by so doing, he or she seeks input from other employees and makes sure their voices are heard.

Servant leaders refuse to put policies, procedures, and the bottom line above their staff. Servant leaders are equipped with the following skills: listening, teamwork, inclusion, high awareness, and persuasiveness. Servant leaders serve as agents for change; they help sustain the culture of the organization by recognizing the urgency in meeting employees' needs and the influence this will have on their performance and satisfaction. A servant leader knows how to obtain commitment from others and how to recognize and use inner potentials to develop and grow employees. Servant leaders believe in motivation and appreciation, and they know there cannot be a productive, effective organization when employees are unhappy. They also believe productivity can be improved or increased only when the needs of both the employees and the organizations are met, that the two must be happy before a successful and meaningful organization can be created.

Transformational Leadership Style

This is commonly seen with leaders who have purpose and direction. This leadership style is about how leaders use their positions and behaviors to develop employees and at the same time affect employees' behaviors through a meaningful and effective working environment. Transformational leaders are motivators, visionaries, and pathfinders. Transformational leaders use communication skills to effectively express vision and direction to employees. They know how to create a collective agreement and build a village of movers and shakers. They know how to use their positions to encourage participation that could lead to meaningful and productive outcomes. They know how to connect their employees' sense of identity with the organization's vision that will produce hope and aspiration for a better future. Transformational leaders know how to use their position to generate can-do attitudes and behaviors among employees and are always looking for new ways to do things. Transformational leaders know that by encouraging, motivating, inspiring, and building lasting positive working relationship, they may reach their destinations faster. According to Bass (1997), transformational leaders understand the power of motivation and use their positions to encourage and inspire others to go beyond the call of duty towards the organizational goals and objectives.

The four areas of transformational leadership are
- purposeful influence;
- intellectual encouragement;
- inspirational motivation; and
- encouraging support.

Directive Leadership Style

A directive leadership style offers control over how and what needs to be done and achieved and allows the leader to provide the employees with specific guidance as to goals, missions, values, and means of achieving these variables and improving on the performance of the organization. Directive leaders ask for feedback and corrective actions when goals are not met. The frequent feedback from the directive leader perspective helps improve performance. Through their feedback, directive leaders are able to better ensure their employees' performance is on track. They are able to provide ongoing assessment on work related activities and assist in the development of timely intervention when employees are not doing well. If use effectively, directive leadership can help with role clarification and responsibilities at the initial stage of the relationship, which often leads to better teamwork and improved productivity. If care is not taken, a directive leadership style can lead to a negative work environment and poor productivity because of its ability to take away employees' individuality, creativity, and willingness to participate.

Authoritarian or Autocratic Leadership Style

This is a style that is not in support of mutual involvement and collective thinking. The practice that is seen here is that the leader makes all decisions without seeking input from employees. This leader believes in *I* more than *we*. Transparency and communication are often not the rule of the game with authoritarian leaders. They see knowledge as power, and because of this they tend to withhold information from their employees. These leaders often use negative reinforcement and punishment to enforce rules and involvement of employees. Instead of promoting a non-punitive culture, they believe in an environment where mistakes and omissions are not tolerated. The leader searches for mistakes at all times and uses this to demoralize employees. These leaders want to be included and informed of all things that are going on in the organization. They always want to have the final say on everything.

Unilateral decision-making is a common method by these leaders. This leadership style, if used frequently, can have an impact on an organization's trust, respect, communication, and behavior.

Transactional Leadership Style

This style makes it possible for the leader to examine the relationship between job performance and desired outcome. They assume employees are responsible for their actions and work. They believe in the classic school of management thought and its important role in shaping behaviors, attitudes, and performance levels. These leaders often use praise, coaching, and support to reinforce a desired behavior. Leading is seen as two-way traffic: you give me this and I'll give you that; they highlight the proper exchange of resources. They develop exchanges or agreements with their followers, pointing out what the followers will receive if they do something right as well as wrong. They recognize the employees' appetite for success and encourage them to achieve any goals they have set for themselves by offering rewards and support, and by sanctioning them if those goals are not met. They often focus on effort-reward relationships and may involve an exchange between employees and the leaders. Transactional leaders tend to work within their organizational cultures following existing rules, procedures, and norms. They are task- and outcome-oriented leaders.

Democratic Leadership Style

This encourages open communication and an open-door policy and encourages employee participation and engagement. These leaders believe relationships are important. This style allows for better accountability, responsibility, and engagement and is a style that could be used to provide quality and meaningful feedback to employees regarding their performance. These leaders are more system oriented and able to look at the global impact of actions and decisions instead of an individual.

Empowering Leadership Style

This is about power sharing for the sake of the organization where the leader shares power with employees by allowing them to participate in the planning and implementation of a decision. It's a style that makes responsibilities and ownership fall on both the leader and the employees. This style makes staff development and support easier for the leader because each member is asked to contribute, participate, and collaborate during the decision-making processes, which in turn could lead to improved self-confidence, awareness, and identification of employees' hidden potentials. It could also bring about individual autonomy, motivation, and improved behavior, which could be used or capitalized on to develop a better culture for the organization. The empowering leaders make work environments more interesting and better for team building and self-actualization. This leadership style makes all necessary provisions available to all employees and allows them to spend more time in the exploration of ideas and how to contribute positively into the organizational growth and development.

The core principle of this style is individuality and potentials. Leaders who utilize this style have seen improvement in the individual professional and personal growth and in outcomes and performances, and more importantly, it has allowed for a workable culture. In this type of culture communication is open, relationships are better, and transparency is valued by all. It is a culture where equal justice under the law is embraced by all leaders within the organization.

Each leadership style has its applicable time and place depending on the organizational culture and the employees who report to you, with no one style being better than another. The effectiveness of each style will depend on the ability of a leader to accurately determine which is appropriate for his or her organization and the ability to effectively implement the characteristics of the chosen style.

However, what we have seen across numerous organizations and industries is that more and more leaders are claiming to be transformational. If transformational leadership is about leaders motivating and inspiring their followers to go beyond the call of duty so that they are willing to put in extra effort on the job, help their coworkers, and engage in other organizationally beneficial activities, it is not surprising to see more and more leaders gravitating toward this style. It can be used to prepare the foundation for long-term changes. Transformational leaders are known for their ability to encourage, motivate, and energize employees to do excellent work that could help prepare a reliable and useful path for the future of the organization.

Because the success of your employees depends largely on your leadership style, it becomes highly imperative for you to have a style that is not only good for the organization and its goals but one that will help in the development and growth of the employees under your leadership. Your role is of great importance to your staff and to the organization because you are the one who will help design, create, and shape the culture of the organization. It's through you that participation and commitment will be made possible. Your ultimate goal is to make sure staff is encouraged to follow group objectives instead of their own personal agendas, which could have a direct implication on the success of the organization.

In selecting or developing a leadership style, you must know that how you react to problems, resolve crises, relate to employees, and reward or punish them are ways in which you will be judged. Your effectiveness will depend on how you can influence and control your employees toward the common final goals and objectives.

The financial position of the organization has a direct correlation with your leadership style. The success of a program or the organization will largely be based on you and your behaviors. You must constantly seek means on how to create a culture that is flexible and open to change, a culture that is conducive to creativity, problem-solving, and risk taking if you want to help the organization to withstand the storm and the waves that are blowing. The storm will be so strong that only those organizations with a strong foundation and pillars will be able to survive it. There is no doubt that you will be challenged and confronted by various factors and problems, but it's expected that you will effectively lead. Which means you will be forced to take bold steps outside the box in order to generate the type of atmosphere that you are looking for: an inspiring and engaging working environment.

The following indicators are helpful identifiers of your leadership style. These indicators are needed for effectiveness, participation, and better organizational performance:

- trustworthiness
- purpose
- empowerment
- creativity
- personal responsibility
- reward and recognition

- appreciation
- accountability
- honesty
- openness
- communication
- understanding
- listening ability
- influence
- ownership
- dependability
- motivation
- respect
- inclusion
- diversity

Apart from the above factors in leadership style effectiveness, there are some other variables, known as leadership theories, that must be considered. There are various types of leadership theories, but this book is going to look at four theories that will be essential for you as a growing leader. They consist of certain qualities that most leaders must be aware of. They are like a pillar that provides foundation and support to a building; they are needed to provide the support that a leader will need when carving out a leadership style that will be used and be effective and relevant as a leader in the organization.

The theories being discussed in this book include the Path-Goal theory of leadership; Vroom-Yetton-Jago decision model; Hersey-Blanchard Situational Leadership theory; and Fiedler's contingency theory of leadership. These four were selected because of their relative influence on the leader and the relationship that must be present between the leader and the employees. They were also selected because they could help provide the needed framework for your leadership style.

Path-Goal Theory of Leadership

This theory could be attributed to the transactional leadership style because of its impact on employee behavior and perception of leadership. The theory talks about leadership behavior that best fits the employee and work environment in order to achieve a goal. With this theory the leader is directly in control by giving directions and supports that are needed by the employees to perform to the expectation of the organization. The interpretation of the theory could be that the leader has a vision or goal as to how to get to the next destination; he or she sees a path and a formula that could be advantageous to the organization and makes all others follow this path. He is like an army commander giving an order to his troops about where and when to take action against the enemy, and he is going to make every employee follow his commands in order to achieve those set goals and expectations. He can force, punish, or reward employees in order to get the task done.

This is when you do what you can as a leader to clear the way for employees to be active in the process of accomplishing the goal. You do this by delineating clearly what needs to be done and provide resources and incentives for those willing to follow your path. You may facilitate the group by appealing to them and their self-esteem and allowing them to enjoy the task at hand. You can be participatory in this case with your employees by taking orders and notes from them. The main reason for using this leadership style is to increase your employees' motivation, empowerment, and satisfaction so they become productive members of the organization.

Vroom-Yetton-Jago Decision Model

This theory looks at how decisions are made in the organization and to assess how the nature of the group, leader, and situations determine the degree to which the group is to be included in the decision-making process. This theory allows you to see how you are making your decision, are you telling them, include them or seeking feedback from employees. In looking at your leadership style, you should be able to tell how decision is made and if employees are involved or included. Decision-making could also depend on the situation; there are some decisions that you have to make because of the time, the nature and the urgency that will not allow you to consult others for their views. There is no one style of decision-making that fits it all, most decisions are based on the situation and the nature of the problem. You as the leader must determine if you are going to be autocratic, consultative, and collaborative when trying to make a decision. It should be noted that good decision always need good human relation and interaction.

Hersey-Blanchard Situational Leadership Theory

This theory operates in the same vein as the contingency theory, where leadership depends on each individual situation and that no single solution fits all or could be considered the best solution to all problems. As a leader you should be able to alter your style to fit any situation at any time. The style to use in each situation will depend on how the leader communicates his or her intention to the employees.

Fiedler's Contingency Theory of Leadership

This theory says effective leadership depends not only on the style of the leader but on the control over a situation and event. It emphasizes the power of relationship, clear direction and goals, and accountability. These three characteristics must be present before a leader can be seen as effective. To determine the type of leadership style to use, the leader must look at the nature of the task and the composition of the group.

As a leader it's important for you to weigh the situation and determine how to approach it in a way that will be beneficial to all employees. If you're dealing with a shortage of staff, your approach will be different. If your employees are new and highly educated and you're meeting them for the first time, your leadership approach will be different than if you already knew them and they are less educated.

Before technology, personal touch was one of the methods used to establish social relationship and understanding and test the leadership competency and ability to lead people. Today the situation is different, the demography is different, and the needs are different. Because of these differences, the leadership style should be different for each occasion. Every situation in the organization will require different approaches and competencies; they will require different styles of communication, relationships, and associations from the leader. It is the adaptability and flexibility of the leader that will determine how people react to his or her demands, controls, and leadership styles.

Points to Remember
- Learn how to lead.
- Understand your behavior.
- Learn how to manage yourself first.
- Refrain from egocentric behavior and thinking.
- Feel secure and confident in yourself.
- Have a vision.
- Positive attitude will serve you well.
- Know how to control your temper.
- Know your people and their different needs.
- Be ethical in your actions and behaviors.

- Always consider others, their feelings, and their thoughts.
- Be respectful.
- Think big and sell big.
- Learn how to be proactive.

Chapter 2
Leadership Development

A large part of my professional career has been spent in health care-related organizations. As a result, there will be several references throughout the book that, while they are health care based, the applied principles are applicable to any industry.

The same challenges faced by health care organizations today are also being faced by many organizations across various industries, ranging from uncertainty due to the ongoing changes to health care policy and laws to the rapid and increasing evolution of information technologies and their application of these technologies to the security of patient information or data. Other major headaches for leaders are the shortage of key health care workers and the high turnover of knowledgeable workers. To be able to cope with all these changes, health care organizations need leaders who are proactive in their actions and, most importantly, who understand and know how to work with knowledgeable workers and their various demands.

Our society tends to use two words interchangeably when describing the leadership role in organizations: *management* and *leadership*. They are not the same, and they have different functions. Management strives for control and predictability while leadership strives to influence and help position the organization for success in this highly competitive environment. The leader looks for change, creativity, and adaptation of new ideas that could be applied strategically to move the organization from the current good status to a great one.

The new health care leader must be futuristic, a vision-driven leader who knows how to inspire a workforce that is dynamic and flexible in behavior and attitude. The new expectations for a leader demand the ability to innovate, mentor, and facilitate by providing positive and inspiring feedback to employees. When we talk about leaders and the ability to create a functioning human relationship with their followers, the following qualities must be present, and if they are practiced and followed as explained in this book, the possibility of creating a nurturing and viable working environment will be higher than for others who struggle with some or all of these qualities.

Transparency

In building human relationships, one thing that your followers must see and feel is transparency. In today's health care environment, transparency means more than simply being honest and loving; it means rendering the decision-making closer to the employees rather than restricted to the boardroom alone. Transparency means the leader's ability to engage employees in strategic decisions while highlighting the organization's responsibility. In health care, transparency is the free flow of information from the boardroom to the cafeteria, a process that allows data and information to be more accessible to every member.

Transparency is about clarity and truth. A transparent leader makes sure there is a free flow of information and that all necessary data and information are made available to all concerned employees trying to make decisions or engage in meaningful and useful dialogue with each other. Transparency means you allow open communication between the leadership and the organization's shareholders.

We have learned through the years that when transparency is part of organizational thinking, there is no room for negativity and bickering between leadership and employees. It helps promote good governance and uphold better accountability. Transparency could also increase employees' perception of the leaders and their leadership styles. When you engage in an open leadership through transparency, you are indirectly contributing to the growth and development of your employees. They become risk takers the organization can depend on for growth and innovation. Leadership transparency helps develop a heightened sense of job responsibility and accountability, which, in turn, influence middle managers to increase their oversight and supervision for better employee performance and productivity.

In contrast to a command-and-control authoritarian leadership style, which is far from being people friendly, this style does not see the value in collaboration, employee participation, and inclusion in decision-making. Control authoritarian leadership style is about power and end results. The leaders that are known with this type of leadership style are task-oriented and bottom line committed. The needs and wants of major players and resources are not of interest to any leader with this type of leadership style.

Transparency in leadership style fosters collaborative leadership that empowers employees to feel that they are contributing to the decision-making process. A transparent leader must

- admit to mistakes and report mistakes in a timely manner;
- refrain from personal gains and rewards;
- make communication open; and
- be easily accessible to employees.

Above all, a transparent leader must encourage two-way communications and always create time to seek employees' concerns.

Transparent leaders should have these core principles as part of their leadership style:

- Your disclosure must be on time. There should be no delay in transparency should be done immediately. Do not wait for weeks, months, or years be you communicate what has happened and what is going to happen.
- Use transparency to grow and develop your employees; do not use it diminish, downgrade, and condemn employees and their viewpoints.
- Use transparency to seek employees' feedback on issues that will or can the organization. This will help promote a sense of belonging and probably move employees closer to you than before.
- Be generous in letting information out. Learn not to hide anything from employees. Remember that anything that is hidden will be revealed soon rather than later, and when it is, it can damage your reputation and image leader.
- Encourage and promote internal and external communication. Open and hon communication helps remove gossip, the promotion of informal leaders, disorientation among employees.

One management theory, Fred E. Fiedler's contingency model, supports the widely known notion that there is no one best way to do anything and that the best method will depend on the situation and time. Your transparency as a leader will definitely depend on the situation at hand. A serious incident will require a thorough investigation before any disclosure can be made. However, it's the leader's function to alert employees of the pending situation without going into details and then to come back later, after the investigation has been concluded, to talk more about the incident.

What a leader cannot do, though, is to say nothing. Saying nothing allows rumors to develop, and rumors are often followed by fear in the absence of sound, accurate, and timely information. We've seen this in various government operations such as the chemical spill that happened in West Virginia in 2014.

The state government did not provide on-time communication about the incident when it first happened; the government waited for days before their first disclosure. The state government used that silent period to collect accurate data and information before making any comment on the leak. The same was true with the Malaysia Airlines jet that disappeared in the open ocean. The differences between these two incidents were the time and nature of communication and the people who were affected.

Based on contingency theory, those in charge in each of these cases did not follow the four principles of transparency, and because of that, the leadership's image was damaged. The disclosure in both incidents was late, there were hidden facts, and the communication was not adequate. When you add all these up, the leaders completely lost their people's trust.

The internal structure of an organization often dictates the type of relationship between the leader and the employees, and organizations that have less turbulence and operate in less stable environments operate more effectively and efficiently because the internal structure of these organizations is less formalized and more decentralized. The leaders of these organizations understand the power of transparency and open democracy. Internal structure should allow for better communication, respect of ideas, and promotion of common goals. Internal structure makes transparency easier; therefore, leaders must know how to create and develop a better working environment and a more productive internal structure.

Professional Example #1

A friend of mine worked for a health care system in the western part of Oregon and was impressed by the high degree of transparency practiced by every member of the leadership team. He told me that during the H1N1 (swine flu) outbreak, despite all the information and lack of information that were common with this outbreak, the way the leadership of this organization handled the situation made it less stressful for every member. He told me the president of this organization held meetings twice a day on this topic, asking employees for information and their help and assistance in preventing this disease from spreading. He was up front with all information that he knew and held back nothing from anyone.

He and his leadership team were out talking to the employees and the customers every day, and every six hours they told them what had been done, how many cases of H1N1 have been treated, and what the hospital was doing to prevent it from spreading. Employees got to know what had been done and what was being done to protect them and their family employees.

According to my colleague, the high level of transparency that the leadership displayed allowed them to handle the outbreak correctly and adequately. There was a collective effort to fight this outbreak. Employees bought in to the leader's vision and strategies on how to treat and prevent the spread of this disease in the organization. It can be seen from this case that the leadership of this organization followed all four principles of transparency

Professional Example #2

Another colleague who works for a different health care organization told me how, during the 2008–2009 financial meltdowns, the hospital leadership used transparency to secure the corporation, diminish fear, and promote a sense of unity in the organization.

As soon as the news of the loss on Wall Street was announced on television, the leader called for an emergency meeting of all stakeholders and informed them of what would be happening in the next few days, weeks, and months and what this could mean for their retirement and savings. There were several meetings between the leadership and employees on this national problem. The leader used the meeting to share national and local news about the financial situation with employees. Most of the time he allowed for an open forum and dialogue, which allowed each member and each group of employees to ask him questions. He also brought to these meetings financial advisers whom the employees could talk to about their concerns and questions. His response was immediate, the transparency was used to educate and improve employees' knowledge on financial management, and above all, the communication was excellent.

The advantages of this open management and transparency were more engaged employees, more risk takers, and more committed employees— employees who believe in their leaders based on their experience and history. The leader used his openness to promote organizational stewardship and ownership. The action helped increase the accountability and dependability of employees.

Professional Example #3

I have worked and befriended people that have worked under various leaders and have told me their various experiences when working for leaders that were closed in their actions and practice less transparency in their leadership programs. There was a health care organization in my town, which happened to be the only midsize hospital in the area. This hospital has been the center pillar for quality health care services to the region. Unfortunately for this organization, it had huge leadership problems. One of these problems was lack of transparency.

Communication and information flow was a difficult thing in this organization. Looking to its history, the negative impacts of poor transparency could be seen among employees and customers.

It was customary for leaders to lie to employees; if employees didn't know how to lie or know how to cover up for the leadership, they would not survive there. The nurse leader was known for her manipulative and deceiving behaviors. She knew how to come up with a story. I was told by a colleague who used to work there that most of the time they were not made aware of what was going to happen, what had happened, and why it happened. People were informed on a need to know basis and asked to follow directives with little explanation as to expected outcome of directive or why the directive was being issued.

The impact of this poor transparency could be seen on the score card. Different quality indicators weren't impressive. Employee morale, engagement, and perception of leadership all got negative scores.

In her further explanation, this friend explained that other employees were not happy with their leaders. Productivity, morale, and creativity were low. There used to be meaningful, helpful, and informative employee forum meetings where employees were told what was going on and what they should be expecting.

Having up-front information allows employees to work more efficiently and with higher morale. They know what is expected of them, how their work fits into the organizational goals, and they feel valued and trusted because their employer shared with them.

With current leaders most forums went from full and useful to empty and irrelevant to the employees. The result of this lack of transparency could also be seen in the way employees react to leadership directions and instructions. There was empathy and disillusion among employees. The organization lost most of its brilliant talent, created a poor image for itself, and lost the competitive edge it used to have among other health care organizations. The overall retention rate of this hospital went from been favorable to less favorable. This hospital witnessed a huge increase in employees leaving the organization for similar organizations within the area or state. Almost all the employees lost the belief and confidence in the leadership and their management styles.

As a developing leader it's important to have a clear understanding of all the positives and negatives of poor and lacking organizational leadership transparency. Transparency is more than being honest and open about your actions and behaviors as a leader. To be effective, your transparency requires your total commitment and openness. You must be willing to share with staff and other employees your processes, analyses, targets, and reasons why. It requires you to explain more vividly how you came to your conclusions. You must also remember that it's not you alone who needs to have a clear understanding of how you came to your conclusions; those you're leading also need the same understanding of how you arrived at these conclusions. What you gain from this approach is that your transparency gives you a clear understanding and awareness of your plans and actions and your potential for success or failure.

Being transparent means, you see assistance in most areas and are in need of input and suggestions. It's a behavior that helps showcase your leadership style to your employees; it tells them who you are and that you are a leader who understands the principle of contingency theory (no single solution for any problem) and that you do not know it all. The contingency theory in leadership means the leaders believe that there is no best way to organize, lead, and make decisions for the organization. The main point is that all decisions and actions of a leader depend on various internal and external circumstances. In practice, it's this circumstance that often dictates the direction and action of a leader.

In building better relationships with your employees, it's important for you as leader to have a policy of no secrets and no cover up. Your being transparent could help diminish fear, and all the unknowns that comes with closed and secret objectives. Your employees want to follow you; they want to believe you and help you achieve your goals and aspirations for the organization. These can only happen when they know there is no hidden agenda. My advice for you as a growing leader is to always let your yes mean yes, say what you know, and when you don't know, let them be aware of this. Don't forget to clarify and answer their questions when you finally know.

Your organization is looking for you to help create a culture that is motivating and encouraging, so you need to improve and make transparency one of your key points for success. Transparency will help you build more meaningful relationships with your employees because any inspiring and effective leaders should know that treating employees as human beings can help in creating a culture that will be positive, rewarding, and good for the organization.

Points to Remember

Developing a better working culture will require effective internal communications.

- Transparency behavior by the leader is needed internally and externally. Transparency helps eliminate gossip and rumors. It helps promote creative
- ideas and associations.
- Transparency can help the leader explain roles and responsibilities to employees and can help with accountability and behavioral modification for employees.
- Transparency is a leadership tool that can be used to enhance individual interactions and job performance.
- Transparency can be used by the leader to foster a sustainable organization, strong and effective partnerships with outside stakeholders, and drive a better and more meaningful competitive advantage for the organization.

Chapter 3
Leadership Awareness

When I'm alone in my little world, I always think about things that keep people from achieving their goals and being successful. Everyone defines success differently, but everyone wants to be successful. Whether that means being able to provide for your family, or making a certain salary, or having a desired work-life balance and flexibility, or rising through the ranks of your organization to a desired position, whatever defines success for you will ultimately inform what motivates you to achieve it. I strongly believe that we are all equipped with some types of skills and talents that can help us with our goals and ambitions in life, and the only difference is how we creatively tap into this well of internal resources that we have been provided by our creator. Have you ever thought about why some people succeed and others don't? The motivation theory talked about intrinsic and extrinsic factors for motivation, and after looking at these two factors, I came to the conclusion that the inner or intrinsic factors can be the difference between those that succeed and those that do not. Some people are highly motivated while others are not as motivated as they should because of one reason or another. The lack of motivation can be due to low self-esteem, lack of belief in themselves, or having no idea as to what their potentials are and the possibilities that are within their reach.

In order to be able to overcome some of these hindrances for growth and development, it's important for any leaders to know what and where his or her potentials are and how to use these potentials for both personal and organizational development. To help provide some useful answers to some of these problems, I will touch on some leadership techniques that can be utilized to help the leaders discover hidden talents. We look at the power of leadership and self-awareness on the organization, the employees, and the overall outcomes. It's important for you as the leader to perform a self-awareness assessment and for you to encourage your organization with its awareness. Through your self-awareness you will be able to discover your strengths and weaknesses and areas of opportunities. As a growing leader, knowing your potentials and weaknesses will definitely shape the way you lead and will help bring about a successful and efficient organization. You need to know what you would like to accomplish, what skills are required to do this, and what the motives are for doing this. After you have developed and discovered your motives, it will be easy for you to develop your action plans and steps that you will have to take in order for you to be able to achieve your initial plans and goals.

Self-awareness is an honest understanding of your own values, desires, thought patterns, motivations, goals, ambitions, emotional responses, strengths, weaknesses, and effects on others. Your self-awareness will allow you to form, manage your own behavior, and improve your interactions and relationships with others, perhaps most importantly your employees. Knowing yourself is a tool that will help you be an effective leader and will improve your circle of influence among your peers and within the organization. Whether you are a new leader in your organization or have been in a leadership for some time, having a deeper understanding of yourself and the organization is a comparative advantage that will benefit you and your team.

Your understanding of the environment and the culture of the organization will enable you to understand yourself and your employees' behavior and help you handle your emotions well and develop a high tolerance skill for others. Your self-awareness will enable you to be a passionate, compassionate, and concerned leader. You will have a better understanding of others and what should be done to improve relationships with them. You will also be able to inspire and influence them for common goals for the organization. To have an understanding of self can facilitate the quick development of a better culture for the organization.

The main purpose for leadership awareness is to help you be an effective leader, to have a clear understanding of what it is to be a leader, and to be able to model behaviors that are insightful and encouraging to other employees. Your self-examination would reveal those behaviors that are positive and are needed for the growth of the organization, as well as those of the employees. It will enable you to be conscious of behaviors that are barriers to employee productivity.

To have a full understanding of your role as a leader, it's important to do a leadership self-awareness assessment at regular intervals during your career. There are a number of online resources through which an assessment can be taken. These assessments involve self-introspection, self-reflection, and self-encouragement. Some sample assessment tools include the Myers-Briggs Type

Indicator (MBTI) and a personality assessment. Okay

Self-introspection involves defining what your goals are and what motivates you. Self-reflection involves looking at yourself over your career in various positive and not so positive professional situations and identifying what you did well that led to positive outcomes, and what you did not so well that you can have done differently for a better outcome. Lastly, self-encouragement involves believing in yourself as a leader, investing in yourself to be an even better leader, and transferring that encouragement to your team.

Your role is more than budgeting and scheduling; it involves your ability to dialogue with people effectively, to negotiate, to listen, to influence, to inspire, and to mobilize employees toward the organization's goals, mission, vision, and objectives. Leadership assessment is highly recommended for any new leader, because without self-awareness, you will not be able to recognize that your behaviors and attitudes are having an impact on the organization and its employees' ability to perform to their maximum potentials.

The questions below will test your ability to lead your organization into the next level. They are to help you assess your management style and leadership skills. All these questions are centered on the following core curriculum on leadership. Your score in each of these categories would be an indication of areas where you need to spend more of your resources and time. These categories are

- communication and relationship;
- leadership skills and knowledge;
- overall knowledge of your organization; and
- talent management.

Communication and Relationship

- What is my value?
- What is my biggest asset or strength?
- What are my weaknesses?
- What do I think about me and the rest of the organization?
- What do I think about my relationship with others, and am I build collaborative relationships with others?
- How do I react to new ideas and suggestions?
- How do I take and give feedback?
- How do I communicate with people?
- What are my best and worst habits?

Leadership Skills and Knowledge

- What are the things that are most meaningful to me?
- Do I value people, and do people know that I value them?

- How do I engage others and respond to their needs?
- How am I growing, and how am I helping others to grow?
- Am I engaging myself positively?
- What influence do I have on people and their level of engagement?
- What are some identified roadblocks and what am I doing to remove them?
- How do I perceive others and their moral obligations?
- What is motivation mean to me, and am I doing enough to help create organizational climate that facilitates individual motivation?
- Have I done enough to help communicate the vision and mission?

What Are My Team-Building Techniques, and Are They Effective?

- Am I fostering an environment of mutual trust?
- Am I supporting and mentoring high-potential talent?
- What am I doing to help create an organizational culture that values supports diversity?
- What am I doing to help promote and enhance sound professional or responsibilities, and accountability?
- How am I contributing to professional knowledge and evidence?

Talent Management

- How am I encouraging networking among coworkers?
- What support services have I provided to employees?
- How do I help promote critical thinking and problem-solving skills?
- What is my recruitment and retention plan? How is this

helping organization?
- What are my employee satisfaction measurements and improvement techniques?
- How am I evaluating and managing employee efficiency and productivity?
- What am I doing to include staff in decision-making?
- How do I manage and develop employee performance systems that are u friendly and promote involvement of employees in the process?

My advice to you as you read this is to take your time to write your answers. Writing down important information helps to make it more concrete and less abstract. It gives you something to refer back to and relieves your mind of the difficult task of trying to remember every response you have to the questions in the assessment tool.

Emphasizing your strengths also helps employees develop their strengths. Your self-awareness will always guide you in decision-making, relationship building, and team building. Your ability to face a new challenge will be less difficult, less strenuous, and less discouraging. You'll be able to build a team of the future, which is made up of risk-taking employees. Your positive image and perception of things around you can help you develop a culture that is engaging and impressive. Your positive attitude can produce a workforce that is full of positive thinkers who have better interrelationships and solid human relations, which can eventually produce desired positive outcomes for the organization.

Professional Example #4

A customer of an organization I once worked for provided me with some information regarding his boss. It was disheartening for me to find out that we had people like this boss in our partnering organizations, despite all the leadership training that we have invested in through various learning centers. He said his boss had a negative attitude toward every new thing that was being introduced in the organization. He said his comments on everything were always negative and not encouraging to his team. This boss saw everything from his own narrow viewpoint, took feedback as an attack, and had terrible interpersonal skills. To make things worse, this boss's attitude and behavior in meetings and at any gathering were equally bad. He thought people liked him, and were friendly to him, not knowing they didn't like him because of his negative behavior. This boss couldn't hold a meaningful conversation without saying bad words. He was known for his lack of knowledge on major issues facing the organization. He had a poor retention rate, and no new employees wanted to work with him.

The department had a poor reputation because of this boss's behavior and attitude. With so much negativity surrounding him, it was difficult for him to have strong, dependable relationships with his employees, which definitely affected the life of the department and those employees who wanted to work there. He failed all the principles on leadership because he did not take the time to do a self-awareness and self-assessment to find out what he needed to improve on to help improve the organization.

Self-awareness assessments are there to help shed new insights into issues that we may not know are bad or going bad. Toxic behavior will not bring positive human relation. It's only when you as a leader recognize the need for change that you will be able to help the organization with its vision, mission, programs and efforts. When we are able to change our old held beliefs, we will be able to change our thinking as well. When this happens, we will be able to forge a relationship that is solid and meaningful to the overall growth of the organization. The more aware you are of yourself and your leadership style, the more influential you are, and the more productive you will be. Your positive outlook will have a positive impact on your followers, and this can also motivate them to be more energize and insightful. As was previously stated, it's critical to your success to do your awareness assessment at regular intervals, and begin to tap into your strengths and work to improve on your weaknesses.

To be relevant to the organization, you must be seen as a team player. This is what your self-assessment will do for you. Self-assessment and self-awareness will enable you to know how to relate to and work with people and not be deep in the silo mentality type of management. Silo mentality defines a management style that regards the department as a separate entity, as opposed to a vital part of a machine comprised of interdependent parts that work together for a common goal. Overall, a silo mentality often leads to departmental isolation and a lack of cooperation between departments and other members of the organization.

Points to Remember

- Know how to engage in self-reflection.
- Always display character strengths of leadership and openness in your interactions with your employees.
- Know how to assess and manage your employees.
- Focus your energy on positive behaviors of your employees and use their strengths to grow them.
- Learn how to customize and individualize your approach and feedback to your employees.
- Be visible, approachable, and show your interest at all times.

Chapter 4
People First, Not Policy

Another key factor to better human relations development is that the most valuable resource is people, and you should try as much as possible to always put employees first by not putting policy and financial outcome as the final destination. The job at hand cannot be done by you alone; therefore, you must always be ready to bring people with you. Understand that the outcome is better when it's done by "us" and not by "I."

According to some human resources theories, people tend to be more loyal to a leader who is compassionate, understanding, and knows how to value employees. The debate surrounding the human resources theorists is that a leader can only be successful when he or she understands the power of appreciation, encouragement, and appreciation of employees' work ethics and productivity.

Why is it so important to not put policy above your employees? The simple answer can be found and linked to the overall performance of the organization, because by ignoring the power of people/employees can negatively impact the organization. When leaders take time to study and understand their employees, the chance of success is very high—higher than for those who tailor their leadership styles on tasks and accomplishments. In their study of subordinates and supervisors' effectiveness, Wu (2012) came to the conclusion that the way the subordinates react to their leaders' request for accommodation, task assistance, obedience, and sacrifice has a direct correlation with the leaders' behaviors, attitudes, and styles.

The leader's behavior matters most when it comes to employees' behavior and performance. Employees tend to work hard for a leader they perceive to be caring and supportive. You as a leader must understand that the employees' perception is a byproduct of their individual beliefs on how the organization as a whole values their contributions and cares about their well-being. If you relate this to your management style and how you see your employees, it's important for you to let your employees know that you care for them and their contributions are valued. Your effectiveness will not be measured by how you always get the job done but as a byproduct of your relationship with your employees. Your use of power and position can determine how your employees perceive you and your leadership style.

Your task as a leader is to get things done through motivation and encouragement, and having employees on the decision-making team can help with this. The five leadership functions (discipline, motivation, planning, staffing, and organizing) can only be done effectively when you know how to efficiently tap into people's skills and hidden talents.

Organization leaders have a significant role to play when it comes to employee motivation and commitment, as well as the predisposition of their entire workforce. Your social intelligence has to radiate among your workers and should allow them to focus and be inspired to perform as directed by you. You must be seen as a role model who encourages and conveys the necessary and desirable attitudes, values, and beliefs for the organization.

People in a community appreciate the strengths in one another, and celebrations for accomplishments abound. In this kind of environment, people are willing to risk being who they can be. This is an environment that appreciates diversity and is safe, where people can make mistakes and learn, develop, and feel good about their growth. You are a coach for most employees and move them from novice to expert.

Serving as a coach helps people to grow and to develop new skills. Coaching enhances workplace performance. Employees can feel the energy, the pulse of learning. There is a willingness to take risks and a feeling of moving forward. Coaching helps identify a desired future state and makes it possible for the manager to paint a picture. What makes this picture magical is how each member of the team is included on the canvas. No one is left out. The team obtains a better picture of where it's going and why. They see how they add value, helping the entire organization to succeed. They focus more energy on the future than on the past.

Leaders coach so their employees will be effective and successful in the future. New skills are acquired and practiced, with the expectation of enhancing future growth. A coach is like a diamond miner. He hires a "diamond in the rough," a person with potential but must be encouraged to attempt new behaviors, to practice, to get feedback, and to practice some more.

A coach is also like a lighthouse keeper, whose job is to bring ships on the open seas to safety during storms. The coach provides direction and closes scrutiny and holds up a mirror, rather frequently, and reflects reality. Some people work hard at not seeing reality, so they miss being all they can be. They settle for an existence, which is much safer but not really as fulfilling.

The coach does all she can do to help people "see it the way it is." This honesty helps employees engage in an inner dialogue with themselves so they experience significant amounts of self-honesty. I would think a patient would appreciate having someone care for him or her who is aware and know how to tap into individual strengths and weaknesses, by working on maintaining the strengths and turning the weaknesses into skills.

Coaches help people to move forward by being positive and focus on the progress that has been achieved. Be patient. Look for the good. Make no comparisons. Paint a picture of the future, and then help every staff member see how she will make a significant contribution in reaching the team's established goals. People need to work toward goals, standards, and behavioral criteria/expectations. This behavior requires feedback and follow-up. People need to hear how they are doing now (feedback), and they need to know that you, the leader, will be meeting with them in the future to see how everything is going (follow-up). As you, the coach, hold people accountable, individual employees will learn to hold themselves accountable. Employees can monitor their own behavior to make sure they are doing all they can. Self-monitoring reduces the need for micromanagement by the leader.

One thing you must look for at the initial stage of your relationship with your employees is loyalty. Loyalty means your employees are ready to travel with you, ready to take the next steps, and finally, ready to improve comprehension on the direction and vision you have for the organization. Every successful organization has one common denominator, and that is employee loyalty, which can be seen as a final product of managers' leadership styles and behaviors. Loyalty is a positive sign for good and better manager/employee relationship.

Putting people first is a good strategy that can help you on your leadership journey. The people you lead must see you as a mentor and coach at all times. They must know you will be there for them when there is a need for your support and leadership. One dominant catalyst to an employee's loyalty is leader support. When employees feel your support and are being supported by you, they will reciprocate by demonstrating positive work habits, attitudes, and behaviors toward your goals and objectives. Their perception of support will energize them to be more proactive and dedicated to the organization. This may also allow them to help you in the creation and fostering of a positive and engaging culture for the organization.

As a leader with a growing skill set, it's important not to put your personal ambitions and gains above your employees' needs.

The policy and financial outcome are there to be followed and they should be reinforced and enhanced into the organization's behavioral standards and values. You must let your people know you genuinely care for their well-being and professional growth and development. This can be exemplified by asking your employees what their professional goals are, and then together coming up with ways that you can support them to achieve those goals. For example, if an employee has educational goals, perhaps they can be allowed to leave an hour earlier on the days they have classes and then can make up the hour on other days. Another example would be by providing continuous training and professional development opportunities both onsite and off. It's most common for such conversations about goals to be held during annual employee evaluations.

It's important that you view employees as one of the greatest assets you have. Their voices can help you maintain and sustain productivity and an innovative workforce. Your goal is to be a servant leader. According to Carter (2013), "Servant leadership is a leadership philosophy that addresses the concerns of ethics, customer experience, and employee engagement while creating a unique organizational culture, where both leaders and followers unite to reach organizational goals without positional or authoritative power."

People must always be your focus and should always take precedence over policy and fiscal outcome. Your employees are looking for a leader who is always ready to invest in them in an effort to help build a solid and viable organization. Your main goal as a leader is to continue to look at how to help your employees on their journey for professional growth and development.

The authentic leadership theory has been used to suggest that when leaders know and act upon values, beliefs, and strengths, and at the same time spend some resources helping others do the same, employees have a better possibility of moving up within the organization, which has been seen as a positive sign for excellent productivity and performance by employees.

To be able to do this successfully, you must have a direct link to your employees; you must share what you believe in and what you will and won't tolerate. You need fairness, a sense of belonging, dedication, and accountability in the workplace. Practice what you preach and do what you say you will. Be consistent and responsible. The reason most leaders fail is because they neglect to follow their own policies. They fail because accountability, responsibility, and ownership mean nothing to them. Known that nobody wakes up in the morning and says to himself or herself, "I am going to work today to perform badly." Most people look for improvement in their work and are happy to come to work with new energy and look for new opportunities, and most importantly, they are happy to be part of a progressive organization. What often happens is that a negative work environment takes away their energy and optimism.

It's important for you to know that when you are fair in your actions, deliberations, and reactions, your employees will repay you by giving you their best. Your behavior and management style will help create and foster a happy and nurturing work environment. You must help create this culture by being fair and committed to the same principles.

As a leader, it's nice to be friendly to your subordinates and to know that most people usually want to do a good job. Make expectations clear and act accordingly by holding them accountable.

Another thing to remember is that every member of your team has needs and wants, and until these needs and wants are met, they will not be okay with your leadership. Your job is to let them know that you care for them and their needs. You should always be looking for areas of opportunity for them at all times. Find out from them about their growth needs, their professional needs and don't hesitate to be personal in your bid of finding out how to meet their needs. Needs may not be only about your employees alone but also of their family, and until these needs are resolve, you will not be able to get their full attention.

The next step in your efforts to meet employees' needs is to be visible and present at all times. You cannot be as effective as you would like to be if you're not visible and present enough to be seen by your employees. As a unit manager, I always made sure my office was the last place for me to be during my unit's busiest time. I was on the floor with my employees, answering patients' call lights, helping move and reposition patients. My job was to provide assistance, talking to the doctors for orders, or calling for wheelchairs and food trays for our patients. I also helped with discharges and admission of new patients.

You cannot be an effective leader if you are not connecting with and helping your employees when the workload is higher than expected. Your presence will also enable you to get to know your employees. You will be able to see and hear what their daily needs are and what you can do to help with some of these problems. You need to find time in your busy schedule to be with your employees. This will allow you to get to know them and the work they do on a daily basis. In your role as manager, taking time to be with employees and helping meet some of their needs can have a positive and lasting impact on the organization. It can help change their perception and impression of both the organization and the leadership, and most importantly, it can help with their loyalty and dedication to the organization and its overall goals and objectives.

I was successful when I was a unit manager because of this approach. I saw improvements in my staff's performance, in their relationships with each other, and to our customers. The unit retention rate was very high and the vacancy rate was lower compared to other similar units. They were loyal to the goals we set for the unit, and we were able to help the organization with its goals and objectives as well.

The irony was that people always asked me how I did it, and I replied that I did not do anything; all I did was providing direction and leadership and made myself available. I made it my duty to spend time with my employees, listened to their concerns, and helped them navigate the system.

In your role as manager it's expected that you will use your position to influence employees toward the realization of the organizational goals and objectives. You will only be successful with this when your management style is compatible with the motivational needs of your employees. I was told a long time ago that the degree of productivity is directly related to the leadership effectiveness. The most motivated employees are usually those who are lucky to be working for a highly motivated leader. My experience as a nurse leader has shown me this, and I can tell you that it's good to be motivated and to be a listener.

Meeting your employees' needs can open doors to greater success because of how employees see their role in the organization. You should know that motivated and satisfied employees can ensure the survival and growth of your organization because of the strong influence your behavior, supports, and coaching have on them and on their performance, which is the sole reason why it's very important not to put policy or financial outcome before your people. If you take time to understand them and meet them at the point of their needs, they in turn will help you in the realization of your goals and objectives. You can also do this by being accessible to them, practice an open-door policy, be present on the unit, make rounds, and be involved. For you to be able to assess your members effectively, you need to have a feedback mechanism in place. Promote positive feedback in your department and learn how to receive and offer positive feedback. You can do this also by making communication pain free by setting up a place on the internal network where employees can offer suggestions and still maintain their confidentiality.

Professional Example #5

I worked for an organization when I was a nurse manager some years ago that had a clear understanding of the importance of keeping people first. It's the policy of this organization that all senior leadership should make rounds on their designated and assigned units. The executive made a conscious decision to have all his leaders maintain a presence in every department, making sure employees have a deep knowledge of what is going on in the organization. I was a nurse manager of one of the departments, and I can tell you that my staff was always looking forward to meeting our designated executive leader. This individual would be on the floor, listening to and answering questions, and at the same time using the occasion to tell staff about the latest developments in the organization. This practice was successful to the extent that most of us in middle management incorporate this practice into our daily routine. Employee morale was up, retention and recruitment were better, and the financial outcome for the organization was excellent.

Another thing we did is what we call reward and recognition. Every member of the leadership and middle management had to honor five employees of his or her team every week. The names were sent to the service excellence department for further action. What followed was a thank you letter from the president of the organization to these employees. The managers were instructed to send birthday and anniversary cards to employees and to thank them for their service and contribution to the organization.

What this organization and its leaders are doing is putting people first. The organization understands the principle of needs and how to meet these needs, and also knows that there cannot be any happy and satisfied customers when there are no happy and satisfied employees. The organization recognized the dilemma of not making the workforce inviting and its people interested and inspired. Through motivation, accommodation, visibility, and accountability, this organization was able to foster and sustain a viable company. Employee loyalty was better and the dedication to the organization's goals and objectives was improved.

Professional Example #6

A friend of mine used to reside in the same community. He always had a story to tell about his organization and its leadership. He was unhappy and unwilling to do anything for this organization because of the way people have been treated by the leaders, who had no respect for the employees. They were treated poorly, and there were no thank you for their work.

The most important point of his story was the way managers have been treated. He told me the nurse leader had no respect for any of her managers; she talked down to them, she insulted them, and she provided little or no support. This was also true about the way she saw the entire nursing staff. There was no recognition from her, no thank you, and no mention of any good things that these nurses might have done. All her energy was devoted to negative things.

The impact of this behavior by this nurse leader could be felt throughout the organization. The worst thing was that she was known for rewarding the wrong people—those who were in her camp, who lied to her, who were lazy and had no interest of the organization at heart.

The impact this leader's behavior had could be observed when interacting with the customers. Most of the employees were unhappy, not loyal, and not satisfied with the way they were being treated. If she understood the power of people, she would have changed her leadership style. However, it was glaringly obvious that this nurse leader had no clue about her roles and functions in the organization. She did not understand the power of human factors to the final outcome. My friend told me this organization has a revolving door when it comes to staff retention because it's very difficult to work there.

Result of this behavior of putting policy first can vary, from poor employee morale, poor quality indicators and performance, low employee engagement, and above all, no commitment to goals. Those employees did not have any reason to be supportive of the organization's goals and objectives. There was no leadership support, no motivation, no encouragement, and no direction. All these necessary characteristics of a people-first organization were absent but provided an opportunity for a new way of thinking. A new view and perception needed to be developed to improve employee dedication. In its current state, employees' dedication to the course was not there, which eventually brought about poor productivity and lack of loyalty to the organization.

As a new leader, building solid relation with your employees is important and significant and should be your main goal. Human relations must be based on mutual understanding of needs and appreciation of efforts. Take time to know your people; get to know their work, their worries, and their concerns as this will enable you to have a meaningful plan on how to foster a better working environment and a performing culture.

Points to Remember

An effective leader has open communication that involves both listening to their employees as well as giving information and feedback that leads to their professional growth and development.
- An effective leader is visible and has a presence within their department within their organization.
- An effective leader is dedicated to his employees and respects them.

- An effective leader is engaged and knows how to tap into the potential of members.
- An effective leader sets measurable and objectionable goals for organization.
- An effective leader understands the power of human capital and helps foster environment that will encourage equal and undivided loyalty to organization.
- An effective leader always find ways of meeting employees' needs with jeopardizing the quality of the product.

Chapter 5
Learn to Listen and Communicate

Another essential part of your job is to lead the organization to the next level at every stage of its operation. This is only possible by taking time to understand the culture. Your initial task as a growing leader is to understand the culture and that of employees. As a leader, in order to remain relevant and effective you must keep informed about the ways your organization and its culture are changing. Knowing these things will prepare you for the tasks ahead and will allow you to have a clear understanding of the people and principles. The organizational culture will tell you more about the organization, it will disclose to you the internal structure of the organization and how this structure is used in fulfilling the organization's goals and aspiration. The culture will tell you how this internal structure has been used to create independent minds and practices.

Understanding the culture and the internal structure can also be a tool that you can use to understand the relationship among employees, and between employees and management. For you to be able to do this effectively, it's important to examine how internal structure has been used to produce better communication with employees. This chapter will look at communication and listening skills and what they meant to the leader's effectiveness and efficiency.

Communication

Communication is a major skill for any leader. It can serve as a catalyst for a better organization. The market environment is not static; it's a changing and revolving environment, and to be competitive in it and be relevant you have to know how to bring your key resources with you. Without them it will be difficult to maintain a competitive edge in the marketplace.

One key element that can help you with this task is communication. Internal communication is necessary for greater employee satisfaction and better organizational performance.

There are different communications styles and methods that like the contingency theory where the benefit of one solution over another is contingent upon the situation, each style and method will be more appropriate in one situation than others.

Communication Styles

Upward Communication: This is when the leader encourages participation of members in communication. This can be done in group settings, on open forums, or during staff meetings. This form of communication gives room for equal contribution and participation by everyone. The merits of this form of communication outweigh its disadvantages. One advantage is a sense of belonging. Another is feeling valued by the leader and the organization. Disadvantages come in the form of disengagement, dissociation, and frustration.

Downward Communication: This is when the leader uses every means to pass on messages to the followers. This form of communication reinforces the position and authority of the leader. This can be in the form of e-mail messages, memos, one-on-one meetings, and group settings.

Due to the volatility of the environment, the need for better communication has never been more important than now. You need to develop a better communication system that will help you with information sharing. Often time, poor communication brings disconnects between the goals and the implementing processes that is necessary to involve employees. It must be understood that your success as a leader will depend on how well you are communicating with your employees. The internal communication should not be done by you alone. It should be something that is embraced by everybody. The internal structure should allow for two-way types of communication. Your communication should be a continuous dialogue between you and your employees and should be used to define the future direction of the organization. Your communication should be meaningful and objective and should always include your employees.

Learning organizations are known for better communication between employees because of their ability to remove potential obstacles and barriers. They know good communication links the various managerial levels and affects efficiency and productivity. They also know that poor communications can result in conflicts and grievances, poor outcomes, and less meaningful relationships with employees. Your communication will help you with your goals and objectives and will help your employees have a clear understanding of what you stand for and where you're taking them. A comprehensive understanding of your values and philosophies will depend on how information flows in the organization and how easy it is to receive information from you, the leader.

If your employees find it difficult to get information from you, the leader, the probability of not functioning to their capacity is high. It must be understood by the leader that not all employees no or have the instincts on how to ask for information and also where and when to ask for information. You must create a structure that makes this easier for them. Your internal structure should help remove doubt and bad feelings about your leadership style.

According to Erikson (1992), there are five different methods that you can use for your communication. Following these five steps can help prevent misunderstanding of purpose and functions.

1. Work Communication. This is what you will use to communicate all the nee information pertaining to their jobs and functions in the organization. This s will help with clarification and any other things that are not clear to them ab their responsibilities in the organization.
2. News Communication. This is the communication that you will use communicate all the latest information and news. It's this type of information that you are sharing on a regular basis that will enable your employees to for your leadership positively. This can be done through newsletter, magazine and any other internal communication means that are available to you.
3. Manage Communication. This type of communication contains budget issue company policies, memos that regulate the business, laws, and regulations s as environmental regulations, quality regulations, and professional regulation
4. Change Communication. Change communication is based on your intel survey and assessment. This communication should be open and involving. Y need to use this type of communication to ask questions instead of telling them what you what to change. This type of communication should be in dialogue format, whereby employees will be free to ask questions about change. The information to be shared can include information about alter business goals, visions, and strategies.
5. Culture Communication. This type of communication touches on the issues relate to the organization's values, its ethics, and attitudes. These are engines for the entire operation. It's about behavior toward leaders customers, community and coworkers. The role of the organization in community and its ethical responsibilities are discussed when using this type communication.

For your communication to be effective, it has to be

Concrete: Meaning it has to be specific and direct. You must bear in mind that the majority of your employees are from different places and have different cultural backgrounds, which means the interpretation of your message can be different if you are not explicit.

Concentrated Communication: This means you're making your information sharing meaningful to all. This communication is based on issues that are meaningful and relevant to all. It's important that you run away from multiple information sharing meetings. When you overload your employees with information, it's difficult for them to grasp key points of your communication.

Coordinated Communication: When planning for broad-based communication, it's always nice to plan it well. Your communication is meaningful when it's coordinated and formulates a unitary picture of the message. You must have a clear and understandable agenda before you meet with your employees

Consequent Communication: You must use your communication skills to explain cause and effect of behavior and action. People must understand that there are consequences for any negative behaviors or failure to follow rules and regulations as stipulated by the organization.

Contrast Communication: Your information must strive to create contracts that will lead to a dialogue. The employees must have a connection with your message. It must create a link to their past or present experiences. From your communication, employees should be able to reflect on the past exposures and compare them with your present thinking and come up with a meaning that will meet your intended meaning and outcomes.

Through communication, people can determine how authentic you are as a leader. As we know, authentic leaders, according to Avolio and Gardner (2005), have multiple levels of influence in the organization. Authentic leader can enhance an individual's positive moods, while at the organizational level; an authentic leader can help improve the quality of work and relationship within the organization which can lead to a positive perception of leadership by employees. It can also serve as a motivator to increase member enthusiasm, which can provide the most needed intrinsic positive and encouraging motivations, and most importantly, it help improve the organizational image, performance, and recognition both inside and outside the organization.

As a leader, it's important for you to know that the old form of organization has been dropped and a new layer of expectations has been build and developed. The new organization has moved away from the Weber bureaucratic organization of individualistic agenda, a dictatorial management style where all solutions and powers are concentrated in one person, while power was centered on one person alone. The organization you're serving is looking to you to help with morale and productivity, which means it's now your sole responsibility to help foster an environment that is welcoming and embraces cross-functional collaboration and flexibility. The only weapon that can ensure that you achieve these lovely objectives is by been transparent and a communicator. You must realize that the outcome of any communication depends on the nature of relationships between the sender of the message and the receiver. The way your messages are delivered will determine how employees are going to respond or adhere to your instructions. You must be good at all levels of communication. You must be effective when you are delivering a soft message like schedule changes, new hires, or new equipment, and you are expected to be more effective when delivering a hard message like personnel problems, firing of employee, or the closing of a unit or service line. Perception of weakness in a leader can bring or lead to negative responses to you as a leader.

These are things that can help you with communication and the understanding of your messages.
- Take your time before answer on issues or events.
- Always make sure you're being consistent with your messages.
- Seek input from employees, and don't let it be your message alone but a "we" message.
- Allow for employee participation during information sharing.

- Use various channels to communicate and share your ideas with y employees. These are some of the channels:
- focus groups
- staff meetings;
- one on one with the employee
- group meetings
- bulletin boards
- social media
- newspapers/magazines
- e-mail
- texting
- intranet

Managers must understand the power of communication and spend more time communicating with their employees. Your ability to communicate effectively can help in the establishment of the needed relationship between you and your employees. It can also help the organization to survive during the storm. Therefore, it's important for you to understand the significant of your communication and the ability to communicate with your employees. The thing you need to know is that culture and communication are close to each other and they are both needed before any meaningful changes can happen in your organization.

It's your ability to communicate that will help create the kind of culture that you are looking for because communication creates culture and it's the culture that shapes your communication.

For you to be significant in your organization as a new manager or a returning manager, you must know that the manager's communication is the sole key for employee engagement and in the stimulation of employees' creativity. Your communication can help improve loyalty and the ability to know and meet employees' needs for the sake of the organization. Your habit of daily communication with your employees can help facilitate social exchange that can produce excellent personal obligations, appreciation, and trust by your employees; this should always be your goal.

Listening as a Leadership Skill

Apart from being a good communicator, another crucial skill that your employees will be interested in seeing in you is your listening skills, which is a desirable trait. A manager with good listening skills can help improve productivity and satisfaction.

Listening is a behavior that is constantly observed by employees. This is because the act of listening means the leader is perceiving, interpreting, understanding, assigning meaning, reacting to, remembering, and analyzing what is being said by the individual. When all these are done correctly, the chances of providing meaningful and encouraging response is high. A good response can be perceived by the employee as caring and sympathetic manager behavior which is equally good for morale boasting and satisfaction.

Literature has shown that listening actually involve three stages; the sensing, processing and responding stages respectively. In any of these stages, it's important that you let your employee know that you are actively listening, which means you're receiving and processing the message and then using your expertise to provide a response. It's your active listening capability that is going to promote further communication between you and your employee. Your active listening is not only based on the aural messages but on nonverbal messages as well (body language, eye contact, and facial expression and emotion).

What are things to avoid when listening to an employee?
- rushing or being in a hurry (This shows you have no time.)
- typing or engaging in other tasks while the individual is talking to you
- lack of eye contact
- lack of emotion and empathy
- injection or interrupting the employee when talking
- providing solutions before the individual is done with his or her story
- distractions, such as phone, e-mail, or newspaper

Your listening can help you with your engaging culture, can help you improve your relationship with your employees, and finally can help with employee satisfaction and dedication to the course. Listening can help promote a trusting, dependable and reliable employee, while at the same time helping with the overall objective.

Professional Example #7

A customer once told me about his organization (a hospital) and what good communication can mean. It was going through a tough financial period, and the staffing office was putting people on standby, calling them off, and even putting major projects on hold. People were using their saved personal time to make up for the hours they did not work. They were coming up with different rumors every day, saying the hospital had been sold, that the organization was going to lay off multiple people, and that the organization could no longer put money into the retirement fund and instead was taking money out of it to fulfill its monthly payroll obligation.

The leaders in the organization got together and came up with a good plan. The president held multiple town hall meetings where he explained what was going on and also used the forum to answer some of their questions. The customer told me the communication during this otherwise difficult period was excellent; people were informed of what and how the organization was going to deal with each problem. Without a good communication plan, the customer did not think the organization could have overcome the problem the way it did. This is a positive story because the leaders did not hide anything from the employees; they were open and direct and at the same time sought feedback from the employees.

Professional Example #8

I came across a colleague during the 2013 Academy of Management Conference. This gentleman was from Maryland. He told me about his organization and how the leaders turned away from open communication.

Everything in that organization had not been working well for the employees. They were in the dark most of the time and were not privy to know what was going on; the direction and decisions for the organization were being handled by a few employees of the elite society. Decisions were being made with false data, and rumors and lying were encouraged and promoted. To be recognized for your hard work, you had to know how to cover up, how to lie, and most importantly, how to keep your mouth shut. People were let go because they would not give in to the culture of lying and deceit.

The top people in this organization isolated themselves from the rest. They did not promote good communication, and most managers were afraid for their positions. One thing he said that surprised me was how leaders were using different tactics to seek information from employees: intimidation, threats of removal from jobs, and encouraging others to lie about issues and problems. The result of all these behaviors can be seen through poor employee morale, poor customer satisfaction, and poor patient care outcomes. One executive employee was known for her lying behavior, and she was a big manipulator and fact changer. Through her behavior, she had put so many people in trouble, and this was not based on their job performance but on some rumors and false data. Because of the lack of communication, the employees lost their trust in leadership and their plan for the organization.

In building professional relationships, it's important for you as a leader to know how to communicate with and listen to your employees. Your people must feel your human side; they must know that you understand them and that you are working on their concerns and feelings. Human relations that are based on good communication makes leading and following easier for everybody, it helps to eliminate gossip, frustration and weariness of employees. Listening skill helps promote better understanding, sense of belonging and appreciation for human feelings. If you know you are not good in any of these two skills, you should begin to work on them now if your goal is to help create a performing culture and happy and dedicated employees for the organization. It must be realized that it's your communication skills as well as your listening capability that will allow you to cope with the frequent changes that are happening in the organization. Your role is to prepare the workforce adequately, so they will be able to help you deal with any changes that might be confronting the organization, changes like global competition and the introduction of new technology.

Points to Remember

As a leader, you must always look for means and ways that will enable you to help your organization in its journey to improve. The goals should be about culture; the type of culture will be determined by your employees and how you relate to them. We know that not all culture can help with the final goals of the organization. Your communication, listening, and relationship skills should lead to the establishment of the following cultures:

- culture of active workers, thinkers, and risk takers with strong creativity skills
- culture that promotes and encourages good habits and discourages bad habits
- culture that promotes and encourages information sharing among employees and information-seeking employees
- culture that believes in basic human values of loving, learning, laughing, and leading
- culture that will always help the organization for continuous improvement

All are possible if you communicate with and listen to your employees—and when you don't underestimate them.

Chapter 6
Be Inclusive

Cultivating Leaders from Within has been looking at various skills that any new leader that is growing in his or her role should possess before he or she can be seen as being effective. We will now look at how decisions are made and what you should know about decision-making processes.

Making decisions is a unique function for any new leader that requires special skills like listening, communicating, inclusion, and respect. Decisions are made for employees to follow; however, a good leader should have a comprehensive understanding of those factors that are necessary for a good decision-making process in the organization.

A good managerial decision will involve every employee; it will be a decision that is made by people for people. As mentioned earlier, this all-inclusive style is called collaborative leadership. A good decision makes use of collective power and thinking. To avoid bad decision-making, the leader must always avoid threats to interpersonal relationships by making sure employees are involved in planning and implementing the new decision. The concept of organizational decision-making is marked by diversity. Many decisions that are made in the organization reflect a wide range of perspectives, experiences, and approaches.

The complexity of organizational decision-making processes demands a broad perspective on communication, involvement, and implementation. The effectiveness of any decision depends on leadership style and behavior and perception of employees. Things that have been noticed to have profound influence on employee when it comes to decision-making are employee perception of leadership influence, their perception on participation, and past history and experiences. Lack of leadership influence often lead to bad decision-making, and most bad decisions are byproduct of poor planning, lack of common goals, weak reasons, and lack of understanding on the part of the employees. When employees are not sure about a decision or if they are not included in the decision-making processes, it can lead to lack of control, insecurity, anxiety, fear and unhappiness; which can indirectly affect the way they relate to you as their leader.

As a leader in the organization, it's important for you to know the significance of your relationship with your employees and how this relationship affects the way they respond to your decisions. The degree of attachment between you and your employees often determines how any decision that is being made is going to be effective and meaningful to the employees. The attachment between you and your employees is valuable because it has implication on how employees react to your call for participation, information sharing, processing and outcomes of your decisions. The decision you make will not be as effective as it should be when there is no attachment, understanding and relationship. What then do you need to have when trying to make decisions that have global implications on the organization?

The first and most important thing is to find the means to include your employees in the decision-making process. Inclusion generally means engaging with others to co-create the future. When you involve your employees, you ask them to help you in the creation of a new organization. This act of inclusion will help with the positive energy that is needed in creating a better future for the organization.

For decisions to be relevant and meaningful they have to involve others and must be involved in the discussion and dialogue that will take place before the decision is made. Inclusion has been shown to improve employees' creativity, innovation, and improves decision-making. The main goal for your inclusive policy is to foster an environment and a workforce where individuals from diverse backgrounds feel valued and respected. This can only be achieved when you invite more people into your board room during decision-making processes.

In their submission on inclusion, Ferdman, Avigdor, Braum, et al. (2010) wrote that inclusion brings feeling valued, sensing that inclusion matters in a positive way, being involved and engaged in the work group, being able to authentically bring the whole self to work, the ability to influence decisionmaking, and feeling safe.

When you include others in the act of decision-making, you're saying they are valued and respected and that their contributions matter. Let us look at the Fiat motor company, an Italian automaker. When its new leader took over this company, the first thing he did was change the way car designs were made, which is usually done by group of hired car designers in the studio. To help improve sales and reputation of the company, he turned the car designing to consumers by asking them for inputs on what a new Fiat car should look like. The result was overwhelming for the organization as more people sent in better and more creative designs. They were able to increase sales and regained some of its competitive advantage in the market (Fiat Organization 2014). (fiat brochure)

Why is it so important to be inclusive? Inclusion and diversity are important because the workforce has changed. The knowledge workers of today are different from before. The workforce is far more diverse in its composition than what it was previously due to changes in demographic, economic, educational, socialization, and orientation factors. In every organization today there are five different generations: baby boomers, generation X, the technology generation, the War World 2 generation, and the millennial working together. There are also different people from different geographical areas. We have people with different cultures, different understandings and experiences.

I remember when I first moved to the United States. I used to be quiet, easygoing, and minded my own business. When I became a licensed registered nurse, I was still in my old habit of keeping to myself. Not too long after I became a registered nurse I learned about teamwork, information sharing, and inclusion. I learned there were people who are hungry for my ideas and knowledge on clinical topics and care delivery. I discovered the power that is in a team work, understanding that care delivery is a community event that cannot be done alone. People are hungry for ideas and they want to share with you their own ideas as well. For example, in health care, including them in the care plan development can be the difference between quick recovery and long recovery. As a leader, it's your caring and your ability to build a strong care community that is going to constitute and form the nucleus of their total experience either as a worker or consumer.

Systems Theories on Inclusion

Systems thinkers in organizations help transcend discipline beyond boundaries. Organizations must have no boundaries but open, organic living —systems that emphasize the dependence on a continual flow of energy and on resources located within the organization (Senge 1990). Systems thinking theory helps shift the criteria from the parts to the whole. The concept of system thinking believes that living systems are integrated wholes, whose properties are to its smaller parts. Organizational activities are the totality of connections among systemic elements used for the unification and interconnection of ideas among employees.

The general system theory, as proposed by von Bertalanffy, allows for systematic investigations into the nature of structure, organizational behavior, and the interdependencies between them. Systems thinking theory facilitates the comprehension of complex organizations by modeling them as united, as rule-governed, and as a comprehensive whole system. Systems thinking theory focuses on the interaction among the interdependent components of a complex organization, with a generality assumption, which states that wholeness is better and more advantageous than the sum of its parts. When leaders look more closely at an organization's environment, they often discover that it consists of various systems and subsystems. The mutual relationships and understanding found among these systems or subsystems help bond people into a whole.

Thornton, Peltier, and Perreault (2004) reported that systems thinking should be a useful way to improve an organization. It should be a helpful tool for initiating organizational change and maintaining continuous improvement within the organization. Decision-making is more effective when others are included in the process. Participation by the whole is an important element of a decision, plan, problem, or opportunity. The best predictors of success or failure are in the social processes used during the decision-making process. These social processes include the degree of involvement and participation by stakeholders in the development of the solution. Literature has shown that when participation fosters decision implementation, there is usually a greater and better outcome and success rate.

Town Halls and Meetings

If you find out that diversity and inclusion are not embedded in your current culture, it's the expectation that you will help by easing into it. Find out from others what they need and want and how they can help in the designing and crafting of a better future for the organization.

Focus Group Meetings or Town Hall Meetings with Your Employees

In these meetings make sure you use the upward communication method instead of downward communication. In upward method there is room for open dialogue, as well as open questioning and answering from both parties. This method makes it easier for employees to contribute to the decision-making and more importantly it allows employees to have the sense of belonging which indirectly helps improve their level of engagement and participation. Inclusion helps build loyalty, ownership and understanding of organization's vision and mission. The leader must understand that the cognitive resources of each employee of the team shall contribute to the company's overall success. This means having more employees with different backgrounds, experiences, and socioeconomic experiences on a team would promote the creativity and decision-making capacity of the team or the organization as a whole. Improved creativity and innovation will occur when leaders understand the power of inclusion and diversity of employees.

You must realize one key factor in inclusion; it's a principle that believes that multiplicity of viewpoints always results in better decision-making skills and creativity. It's a principle that follows ideas that were expressed by contingency theorist that says there is no one best way of leading, that leadership ability to lead effectively is a byproduct of different leadership styles and situations. To be able to work together as a team will depend on the individual's experience, history, education, exposure, and cultural values. When you put all these variables together in your organization, you will end up as a productive organization.

To be successful in your journey as a leader, it's important for you to know that leveraging diversity and inclusion is a necessary skill that you must have and develop. I am saying this because integration is a good leadership behavior that can help you creates a better culture for your employees. It can impact your bottom line; helps increase innovation, and value creation.

As a leader I found out that when I have an openly collaborative environment with my staff, the encounter is usually effective and helps promote discussion around some topics that are important to my staff. The discussion helps deepen critical reflection around topics and issues that my staff perceived to be challenging or sensitive. The advantage that this has on them is that it allows them to understand how communication processes and structures can shape their relationships with each other and their practices, and it helps improve their tolerance for each other, which indirectly influences their acceptance of each other, which cumulate in a better working relationship. They begin to see themselves as a member of a team, a family, and a social organization. My practice of inclusion helps my staff develop a share values and a sense for a common purpose. This is because they have individually made substantial attempts to adapt, learn, change, and communicate better with each other.

In practical terms we know that groups that individual belong to are a source of self-esteem. It provides social identity and a sense of fitting in, which is a catalyst for satisfaction and participation. Many employees are looking for a community where they can connect and relate, and it's your function to make this happen. The only way you can do this effectively is by including them in your thought processes and in the activities of the organization or department. The idea of looking for a team is one of the basic needs of belonging, which says individuals seek inclusion to a group where they are accepted and made to feel secure. You must learn how to create this type of environment for your employees where they feel safe and secure.

As stated earlier, when employees experience inclusion, they feel valued and recognized for their efforts in the organization. This perception of being valued and respected for their contribution often influences their perception on safety, which then opens the door for them to communicate freely by sharing their ideas and viewpoints without fear of intimidation. Every organization is looking for a leader who can help them create an inclusive environment. When you look at the two-factor theory (also known as Herzberg's motivation-hygiene theory), he states that there are hygiene factors, and they have no impact on employee satisfaction. They are things that do not give positive satisfaction or lead to higher motivation, though dissatisfaction results from their absence. Motivators are factors that can help promote and improve satisfaction, loyalty, and engagement of workers in the organization. He cautioned leaders to change from an overreliance on policies and procedures and stop putting these policies above the employees. To be able to help in the creation of an inclusive environment, the manager must begin to foster an environment that promotes inclusiveness and therapeutic relationship because this is the only way you will be able to get to your final destination, which is a productive organization.

Pless and Maak (2004) suggest that an inclusionary approach values the differences in individual employees and leverages diversity in creating a playing field that is raised so that everyone feels supported and performs at his or her best. Inclusionary approach means different perspectives are heard, respected, understood, and integrated into the decision-making processes; differences in opinions and voices are further seen as legitimate avenues for problem-solving and improving organizational performance.

The nursing profession is benefiting from the inclusionary approach to labor management. If you look at those health care organizations that have secured a magnet status (a high honor that any health care organization like hospitals and health centers could be awarded for quality and employee participation), it will be discovered that they all have one thing in common: they all practice a shared governance model in their organization. This stands on the idea that everybody has something to contribute to the growth of the organization. This idea of shared governance empowers all employees of the workforce to have a voice in decision-making and pave the way for creative thinking that will help advance the business and health care mission of the organization. The idea involves teamwork, problem solving, and accountability. The end goal is about employee satisfaction, improved productivity, and quality care delivery.

As a new leader, you're going to benefit more from this type of management model if you apply it correctly to your daily practices. Your daily objective should be about empowerment. It's important that you assist in the creation of an environment that wants to maximize employees' potentials. There are a lot of hidden talents in your organization, and when you're able to prove that you care about their opinions, views, and values, they will be able to display these talents.

As a manager in those days, I embraced shared governance, which gave me more opportunities to discover most of my hidden potential. We had different committees with different employees, and each committee had plans on how the unit could be developed, improved, and maintained. The result of this action and the implementation of shared governance foster unity, create a workplace harmony, and improved staff productivity.

Professional Example #9

I worked for a manager in a local Maryland hospital as a staff nurse. This manager happened to be the first person to introduce me to inclusive management. We did not have shared governance in those days, but our manager always made sure that every member of the team had something to say to get our opinions on her next action steps. She would call a staff meeting and inform us of what she was about to do. She would ask us to think about it and bring our ideas to the next meeting. The staff meeting was not only for day shift employees but for all shifts.

At the next meeting each of us brought our ideas and thoughts to the meeting and deliberated on them together. At the end of each meeting a group would be formed to look at the ideas submitted and come up with some solutions or implementation processes. Decisions were made with the people, not for the people. The result of her management style resulted in a better working environment, less turnover, fewer call-outs, and less conflict between employees. The unit was rated the best for three years in a row by the organization's internal survey result. Nobody wanted to leave this unit because of the way we were treated and valued by her. The patient care that we delivered to our patients was super. It came to a point where doctors and other providers always looked for empty beds in our unit for their patients. We all loved to come to work. The coworkers were good and the workforce provided opportunity for professional growth.

Professional Example #10

As a growing leader I worked for an organization that did not know the difference between diversity issues and inclusion. It looked at these two components the same way. It's common to see leadership talking about inclusion by asking about race, nationality, and gender. Diversity is a national program, and having a diversity program does not mean you're inclusive. In this organization things were done by leadership with no input from other employees. In this organization, employees were often told of new programs, events, and crucial information at the eleventh hour the day of the event. Employees were not privy to know what the leaders were thinking; everything must be in secret, behind a closed door.

One time we were to receive visitors from other parts of the nation; the preparation and other pertinent things were done in isolation by two people, the associate director and one of her trusted, incompetent friends. Both the data gathering and logistics for this visit were done by these two. Their presentation was nothing to write home about, and it was the least interesting presentation to the visitors. It was common for frontline staffers not to know anything about events until it had come and gone. If you did not belong to a special group, you were excluded from any discussion. To be part of the inner working group, you had to look like them, talk like them, or know how to lie to people. One reason this organization was not practicing inclusionary approach was fear and manipulation. The leadership created a fearful working environment and allowed other employees to believe this.

Another thing is manipulation. It was a common practice by some of the top executive employees to manipulate information and data to mimic what they wanted and want they wanted employees to believe. Transparency was not a value that was respected or practiced in this organization.

Most of the time, and because of my position, I was supposed to know certain things and be involved in some planning and implementation. What often happened was that 99 percent of the time, I was not invited or involved in any of the decision-making processes. One day I asked why people were not being included in decision-making. I was told that these employees were not interested, which was a lie, because most people in this organization wanted to be included. To make things worse, one of the leaders always hired people that she could manipulate. If she realized you knew more than she did, were liked by other employees, and were getting things done, she would begin to look for your downfall. She was known to collide with people by asking for information and data that she could use to bring you down. I was a victim of this style when I was moved from my position, and when I asked, I was told by this leader, "When I threw a birthday party, you didn't come, and when I suggested we all go out, you always had things to do." The crazy thing about this type of leadership is that they always have people like them working for them. In this organization, this particular leader had most of the people under her control. This leader did not care if you had experience; she would hire you to put you in position that she knew you were unqualified for because of her selfish behavior.

The result of this type of hidden leadership could be observed everywhere within this organization. Morale was down and poor, the quality of care was substandard, and people were quiet and most of the time refused to contribute anything that might benefit the organization. Employee turnover rate was at the high end, while overtime money had reached the ceiling. People were exiting this organization at an alarming rate. Sick calls were at the highest rate I'd ever seen. People just didn't come to work. The reason for all these negative results was lack of inclusion and listening by the leaders. The environment was so toxic for those who were aggressive and focused.

As you are growing in leadership, make sure you are including more people in your decision-making processes. The only way you will be able to manage effectively is when you understand the power of people, their talents, and their skills. Bringing quality people on board with you can be the very thing that will differentiate you from others leaders.

The organization is looking to see how you can help create enthusiastic workers who are great thinkers, are creative, and are risk takers. You must know that without rebels, the storyline will never change, so you need these rebels on your team. Let them help you change your story. The inclusionary approach will help you cure the diseases that egocentric behaviors can bring to any organization.

To be cured of these diseases, you have to be willing to support your employees, to respect the human aspect of their work, and to see that you are nurturing a therapeutic working relationship with them. Other actions that can help you will be to value employees and their ideas, be a good listener, and foster a good and therapeutic working environment that is a byproduct of effective teamwork and understanding. Your role is to support and direct employees positively and not to be a judge of ideas and behaviors. You should always strive to be a unifier and not a divider.

This table looks at five leadership behaviors and the associated basic leadership style that may help you with your efforts on inclusion

Leadership Skills/Leadership Behaviors

Leadership Skills	Leadership Behaviors
Communication	Demonstrates open and democratic management styles.
Approachability	Humility and humbleness
Adaptability	Discipline: he upholds and value discipline action, discipline thoughts and discipline people
Advocating	His main goal is the people on his team. His goal is centered on people first, not policy
Appreciative	Genuine and authentic style, openness, and likes feedback. Dislikes conflicts

Points to Remember

- Inclusion fosters employee buy-in.
- Inclusion goes a long way in relationship building with your staff.
- Inclusion provides a foundation for employee trust in

leadership.
- Inclusion can increase employee morale when the feedback provided by employees is taken seriously and employees can see the results of their feedback actually implemented.
- Inclusion is crucial to employee retention and job satisfaction.

Chapter 7
Support and Create a Learning Culture

It's an open secret that organizations are facing strong competition, which has created more challenges for the leaders in the organization. The effects of this competition can be seen in the organization's dedication and commitment to overall effectiveness and efficiency. This paradigm shift in the way leaders view quality improvement has resulted to changes in hiring practices and talent management in the organization. For this reason, organizations are now exploiting their employees' full potential. The future of the organization rests on its employees and their willingness to help with its goals and objectives. It's a fact that no organization will be able to survive without a skillful workforce and the initiation of employee activity and without highly engaging and motivated employees.

Providing training to employees will allow the leader and the organization to meet employees' needs. To enhance employee performance, it's the responsibility of the leader to provide training and education that can help improve their competencies. As you know, high competency means high-quality job performance and better productivity. When there is no training and no form of ongoing education, the organization has the tendency not be able to meet the planned targets on effectiveness.

A leader who understands what training, inclusion, and planning will mean to the future of the organization will know how to prepare the organization for eventual changes. Training is the foundation for employees to rest on, while decision-making is the pillar for progressive thinking and creativity of employees; and planning is the overall structure for meaningful dialogue and conversation in the organization. Change is needed and should be about the future of the organization. Leaders are known as agents of change, which means they must always look to the future and help prepare the organization for these changes. For this to happen effectively, the leader must understand the power of people, culture, and environment. All three should be considered before embarking on a planning strategy for the organization or before making any organization-wide decision. It's also important for the leader to embrace data and feedback from people, because a good planning and decision will depend on how the leader utilizes the information and what is being related to the leader via feedback

Learning Culture

Learning in the organization takes place when there is a transfer of knowledge from one individual to another and to the collective body. This knowledge transfer occurs through interactions among different cultures and groups. The main goal is to help facilitate a quick and effective means for information sharing, processing, and interpreting both inside and outside the organization. The basic foundation for effective learning organization is the culture of the organization. This is the reason your attention should always be on how to help the organization in creating a learning culture. A learning culture is one where leadership invests in and promotes the continuous learning of its employees. Doing so sends a clear message to employees that they are valued and expected to be the best at their jobs through continuous learning.

To be proactive in all aspects of human production, it's essential for the organization to have a learning culture because of its contribution to the overall creation of a meaningful and effective organizational culture. A learning culture can also be seen as a performing culture because it's one that is oriented toward the promotion and facilitation of learning by its employees. The learning culture that you are creating will stimulate better learning and sharing of ideas, and will speed the rate of information sharing among employees, which is needed for development and success. We know that organizations that are open to continuous learning will be able to control and prevent crises and to adapt to change more easily and better than those that are not.

Why do you need to support your employees in knowledge creation for an effective learning culture? The answer can be found in the definition that was provided by Senge (1990) on learning organizations, who wrote, "Learning organizations are organizations where people continually expand their capacity to create the results they truly desire, where new and expansive patterns of thinking are nurtured, where collective aspiration is set free, and where people continually learning to see the whole together."

In order for this to happen, your employees must be ready for behavior modification, which means they must be ready to see each other as one, as a unit, and as a body working together for a common goal. As a leader in this organization, you must help employees develop skills that will help them in creating, acquiring, and transferring newly acquired knowledge to each other without holding back on any meaningful and useful information that is needed for the total transformation.

As a nurse manager, one of the things I cherished was teamwork. Teamwork helps in the creation of a performing culture in the organization. On the medical step-down unit, it's important for employees to work together for the sake of the patients and the organization they are representing. Working together brings out specific individual qualities as a team member. If we look at the most successful organizations and teams in the NBA or the NHL or any sports league, it's always the team that works together and values each member that often comes out as champion. The reason for this is that each person sees himself as a member of the team and they are all fighting for the common goal, which is to win the championship.

Another major role that will be expected from you is in the area of communication. For a learning culture to be created there must be no obstacles or barriers. You must be sure your culture and practices are not blocking the flow of communication. People must be able to communicate freely, participate freely, and contribute freely without thinking of any negative response from their leader. The system that is in place must support free communication. For a learning culture to mature, the people must not engage in swallowing and holding behavior, which is when employees do not say what is on their minds and keep information to themselves that is needed for company growth and development.

It's essential that you are seen as a promoter of team learning, shared vision, and system thinking. Your behavior must reflect culture and values. To be able to do this effectively, the following should be your driving forces:

- Vision
- Mission
- Organizational goals
- Strategic goals
- Departmental goals
- Individual goals
- Leadership competencies

Team Learning

In promoting team learning, shared vision, and system thinking, each member of your team must understand the vision and mission of the organization. Vision is the future eye while the mission is the value and principles developed around the vision. It's important for your employees to have a clear understanding of both the organizational and strategic goals before they can help in the formation of a meaningful knowledge transfer and information-sharing culture.

The following must be asked every time you interact with your workforce:
- What are the vision and mission of this organization?
- What are the future goals?
- What are five strategic goals of the company?

When you critically examine these questions on a daily basis, you will be helping in the formation of new dimensions that can help improve employee satisfaction and productivity and you will improve the quality of the workforce.

As a leader in a learning culture and a workforce that is engaging, it will be required of you to provide training. The training must be for new hires and current employees. Ongoing training should be made available to workers, and this should be part of your goal as a leader. Doing this will help prepare your members to be ready for changes and any other things the health care environment might present, if you want to maintain a learning culture. Making training and education available to employees will show your support for their personal growth and professional development, which is crucial in a learning culture. This ongoing training is also needed due to the rapidly changing technologies and for continuous adaptation and retention of a quality and active workforce. For this training to be meaningful and useful to your employees, you must make sure that you are constantly assessing their learning needs.

There cannot be a learning culture if your employees do not know how to work together collaboratively, so it will be expected of you to help in the promotion of a collaborative working environment. Collaboration with others and by working alongside each other will definitely help promote and improve knowledge sharing and transfer between employees. A collaborative learning environment helps in the removal of fear, gossip, and intimidation. This is because the more they work together, the more they learn from each other, which then help to improve knowledge and formation of a more knowledgeable workforce.

Consistency and transparency will be behaviors that you should demonstrate at all time. You should not be seen as someone who is only talk and not doing what he said he was going to do. The single biggest driver of business impact is the strength of an organization's learning culture. There must be a strong commitment to resource allocation, and finance allocation before you can be successful as a leader wanting to create a learning culture. You must support active and independent learning at all time. The change in technology must be met with a new commitment to replace and train employees. You must help create a growth mind-set for the people, which can only manifest with ongoing investment on technology, training, workshops and seminars. You must have a workforce that sees knowledge and learning as part of their job, and what they need to succeed in the organization. Allow employees to be free in their movement by promoting free mobility and knowledge migration from one individual to the others. Allow them to go outside formal reporting lines to discuss ideas and issues with their coworkers without fear. Support them when they fail and reward them when they succeed, because this is going to help with their motivation to do more for the organization and drive them to seek more knowledge. You must let them see your commitment to continuous learning. You can do this by yourself becoming a lifelong learner and continuously monitor outcomes and each employee's level of engagement in learning.

Your job as a leader is to create a working environment that is conducive to learning. The culture of the organization must be the one that enhances good behaviors and discourages negative The existing attitudes, values, and behaviors must allow for continuous learning. Your management style should enhance self-actualization and socialization.

Avoid Being a Micromanager

Micromanaging should be discouraged. As a leader you should understand that micromanaging has a negative impact on productivity and employee engagement. Micromanagement is the act of controlling all aspects of operations without any consideration to employees' feelings and opinions. This often happens when a manager has a distrust relationship with employees and has no faith in their ability to succeed or do the job. This type of relationship cannot lead to a learning culture and knowledge creation.

- Micromanaging can lead to disengagement of employees, which means they are not interested in contributing fully to the success of the organization. Most knowledge workers want to be treated as adults and people who can think independently without any interruption from managers or supervisors. When you promote this type of working relationship, the employees begin to act like cogs in a machine instead of being motivated employees.
- Productivity is likely to be inhibited when you engage yourself in a micromanaging behavior. This is seen when you are spending most of the time correcting and directing employees and pulling them out of the production line. The time they spend with you castigating them can be used effectively by being more productive; the time actually erodes the time devoted to actual production by employees.
- Your leadership style of micromanagement can bring mutiny and rebellion in the organization. What you're likely to see when you micromanage are employees excessively calling out from work and cultivating the habit of tardiness and non-caring behaviors. The impact of this

type of behavior on productivity is significant because employees become antisocial, and significantly reduce their working time, most especially when there is a need for overtime, they are known to decline the offer and go home, leaving others to suffer and the quality of service and care to decrease.

- Micromanagement is a disease that managers should avoid as their leadership and management style. Micromanagement brings low employee morale, high staff turnover, and decreased customer and employee satisfaction. The impact micromanagement has on financial status is often high (high because of poor retention rate, high turnover, and unhappiness of the production staff). The only way you can avoid not to be labeled a micromanager is to find a balance between effectively performing daily obligations and strategically planning for tomorrow for the organization

To avoid all these negative consequences, you can follow what was discussed earlier in this book. You need to work on how to improve communication with employees, be more inclusive in your practices, and get more people involved in tasks by encouraging participation. You need to work on your delegation skills. Promote a just culture as discussed earlier. A just culture sees mistakes as means for growth and development and not as punishment, not as a cutthroat event for the employees. Mistakes should be seen as an important process in the learning experience of employees and as a growing process professionally.

Human Resource Management

Another area that's important as you grow in leadership capability is to work on your hiring practices. To be successful as a leader you need well-qualified and capable employees to help you with your goals and aspirations. Your success as a leader depends on the hard-working, loyal and involved managers and employees. If your aim is to be effective and efficient in your daily interactions and operations, it will be necessary for you to move from the old rigid autocratic style to a friendlier and more contemporary leadership style of management. Your leadership style should support employees, provide them with direction and sense of purpose. You should encourage and create a culture of hope, sense of belonging, and creativity of employees. It must be understood by you that leadership does play a leading role in how employees react to information and goals. We know that employees that are pleased with their manager/leaders with the way they are being treated, valued, and respected feel more attachment with their organizations and their leaders. This form of transformational leadership style can have a significant impact on your ability to manage and lead effectively. Transformational leadership offers the most effective leadership style because of its influence on employee commitment, satisfaction, and loyalty.

A learning culture manager seeks for feedback from employees because of the realization that the glass is not half full. You cannot be seen as an island by your employees, someone who knows it all. When you seek for feedback, you open the organization for a better learning experience by all. You make yourself available and approachable when you accept feedback from employees. You can use this behavior to improve productivity, confidence, self-esteem, and self-actualization. All these will contribute positively to your ability to create and nurture a learning working environment for your employees.

You will need to look for people who are
- willing to embark on a journey that is neither straight nor rough. People that ready to attack all the ills and confusions that have become the norm for m employees and the organization as a whole;

- performing at a high level of their chosen field because these are the people will help you lead and drive any improvement process that can bring the cha that you are looking;
- ready and willing to help drive and implement changes throughout organization on a day-to-day basis, people who are not willing to settle for or tolerate a mediocre behavior and habit that can inhibit the growth development;
- equipped with skills that are needed for negotiation and participation. These people with high persuasion, influencing, and negotiating skills. Those have the appetite and the zeal for better workforce and excellent hum understanding that can help steer the organization through crisis and confusion and bring about desired changes; and
- secure with themselves and have the strengths, assertiveness, and behavioral skills that can be used in the creation of the culture that is not only peaceful enduring.

According to the Gallup survey done among 2,551 managers in the United States, five dimensions of management skills were discovered:
1. motivational
2. assertive
3. accountable
4. personable
5. decisive

Managers with high talent in all these five dimensions are more engaged, are better ambassadors for the brand, and are more likely to focus on strengths than weaknesses. This survey shows that for any manager to be successful in the effort of creating a learning environment, he or she must achieve the higher level in these dimensions. If you look at yourself, what can you say about yourself and your engagement level using these five dimensions?

Professional Example #11

A friend works for a local health care organization in Lansing, MI, and he was so proud of his organization and how it had been supporting professional growth and development of its employees. Each nursing unit allocated money for education and workshops; each unit had a unit-based council where issues pertaining to the employees and the unit were discussed. The manager was supportive, friendly, and approachable. Each employee was allowed to raise his or her hand during meetings.

Respect was one thing the organization adored and promoted. There were set days for learning and sharing among employees. It was common to see leaders in this organization invite community leaders, educators, and philanthropists to come talk to the employees. Politicians were invited to talk about current events and topics. The vice president of patient care services spoke to the nurses every month on different topics, and when she had nothing to share, she invited her executive employees to talk to her nurses. She invited the president and CEO of the organization, the chairman of the Board of Governors, and the chief financial officer to talk on various occasions. This was a learning culture in a learning organization.

I was not surprised when he told me this organization was a magnet hospital. People were happy; customer satisfaction was high, as was employee satisfaction and engagement. The retention rate was higher when compared to neighboring organizations. This organization had a low turnover rate because of this learning environment. The leadership support was another thing that helped in this magnificent achievement by this organization. They communicate, they listen, and they seek feedback. The relationship between leadership and the union partners was excellent.

Professional Example #12

Down the road from where I live is an organization that is quite the opposite of the one where my friend works. This organization has no respect for knowledge and education. In fact, if you're seen as being educated and that you know what you're doing; you become a target for professional persecution. It's a fact that If you are a worker of a different race or minority, and more knowledgeable than them, you have to be concerned about your carrier. In this organization, supervisors, managers, and top executives are the police, looking for mistakes from any minority workers. Their only offense is that they are brilliant, know what they are doing, and are straight in their dealings with others. They achieve and work tirelessly to make the organization better. They know how to follow the rules, policies, and directives, and this is what the leadership of this organization does not what to hear or promote.

Instead of looking for drugs, guns, and knives, these leaders look for things like lateness, rudeness, candor, behavior, and interaction of minority employees. There was a time when, of eighteen employees who were falsely removed from their job, 80 percent were minorities. Black workers were fearful because of this practice by these leaders. The results of this type of leadership style are unhappy employees, high turnover rate, and low morale.

If you examine these two stories, I hope you will make up your mind to help your organization grow and be productive. If you help with engagement, satisfaction, and loyalty, you can achieve positive outcomes. Learn to surround yourself with more knowledge workers, those who have the knowledge and skills that you are looking for, and don't be afraid of their skills. Don't be threatened by their knowledge or education level. Accommodate them and learn how to appreciate them for what they bring to the organization.

In the second story one of the leaders hated knowledge workers, especially those who seemed to know more and know what they're doing. The worst thing she did was surround herself with people of the same feather, local people with no knowledge of what was going on in the profession. Some of these people that she hired to work for her had been fired or laid off from local city hospitals.

As a leader, you must be ready to embrace a learning environment. It must not be toxic. Use your influence to promote knowledge, awareness, and understanding of key elements that are essential for the organization's growth and development.

Begin to ask yourself those questions about what you need to have in place to help promote a leaning organization and culture. Your goal at the end of the day is to help promote the self-esteem of your employees. Having a viable and effective learning culture will definitely help; realizing that self-esteem is the single most important key to a person's behavior, perception of self, and others. High self-esteem is an important factor for high energy and high performance for most employees in any organization.

Points to Remember

- Define your collective goals.
- Hire the best prepared knowledge workers.
- Refuse to surround yourself with like-minded people.
- Allow for free movement of ideas and opinions.
- Be a helper and not a blocker.
- Don't be afraid of knowledge workers, they are there to help you.
- Allow for feedback and know how to benefit from it.
- Constantly build the culture of learning.
- Provide your support.
- Know that failure is a step toward greatness; learn to understand lessons from failure.

Part 2

Chapter 8
Support Creativity

The new technological era and the increase in consumer demands have increased the degree of uncertainty for most organizations across all industries Because of this, we are witnessing how organizations are reacting to some of these uncertainties. What is required is for the organization and its leadership to know how to push employees to develop high levels of creativity in their daily activities and interactions if the goal is to have the courage and energy to weather the storm. This mean that as a leader in the organization, you must develop techniques and behaviors that are capable of helping you in your effort toward innovation.

Creativity in organizations is referred to as the development of employees' ideas that are significantly useful and meaningful to the company's overall mission and vision. Creativity refers to defining new and useful ideas that will be beneficial to the organization and its employees. A creative working environment demands that the leader be supportive, reward, and recognize creativity and encourage the exchange of new ideas, demands clear goals, encourages open dialogue with subordinates, and actively supports the work and ideas of development teams.

In his book, Collins (2001) wrote that great organizations embrace learning and creativity of their employees. They know that creativity is the initial step for a creative mind. In your role as a leader, it must be understood that any environment that foster and embrace creativity will definitely see the result on its return on investment. This is because innovation, particularly in the health care industry, is widely recognized as being critical to the growth and development of the organizations, which can result in a better competitive advantage. Individual innovation means the development, formation, and implementation of new ideas, new thinking, and new focus by employees.

Apart from having good hiring processes in place and an environment that fosters learning and growth of employees, creativity is a positive predictor of a viable organization. Creativity brings innovation and ideas that can separate the organization from its competitors. Creativity can also mean that organization and its employees are able to look at things differently. It can mean a deviation from the present norms and practices and behaviors to new ones. It can also mean that the organization and its employees are looking at products and services from different eyes that are different from what it's now. Creativity can also mean the organization and its employees are taking the first step of looking outside the box.

There's no other way to be competitive and relevant as an organization if employees are not motivated or encouraged to be creative. Creativity as stated above can lead to the production of novel and useful ideas by employees either as an individual or as a group. Creativity provides all necessary layers for innovation in the organization. Because of this, it's important for you as a leader to support your employees and help them discover their hiding potentials that can be used for the growth and for their professional development. The manager must realize that creativity can be instrumental to employees' ability to think and generate ideas for new products, procedures and services.

Cultivating a Creative Work Environment

To help in the development of a creative working environment, the manager must be able to recognize that creative thinking depends to some extent on personality traits, such as independence, self-discipline, orientation toward risk-taking, tolerance for ambiguity, perseverance in the face of frustration, and a relative lack of concern for social approval.

As a leader you should recognize the individual traits and make up because each employee is different. There are some that are more strongly driven and motivated than others by the enjoyment and sense of challenge in their work.

When employees are allowed to dedicate meaningful efforts to fully identify a problem, obtain as much information as possible, and generate numerous ideas and alternatives, solutions that are both novel and useful are more likely to be produced. The leader must see creativity as a single most common factor for innovation, effectiveness and survival of the organization. To support creativity, it's important that the leader assume an important role. The leader must encourage and promote creativity among employees, because of your understanding of each one's capability, and the influence that each has on issues and topics within which creativity can occur.

It's expected that you develop an environment that encourages better performance through motivation and resource availability. It's important to make available resources that can have a dominant influence on employees' creativity. You need to know how and when to motivate them. Your ability to appreciate contributions when they are made will have a lasting impact on employees' ability to think on new ideas. Herzberg's theory on motivation talked about hygiene factors and motivators and their impact on performance and engagement. He wrote that Hygiene factors are those job factors which are essential for existence of motivation at workplace. These do not lead to positive satisfaction for the long-term.

But if these factors are absent or nonexistent, then they lead to dissatisfaction. In other words, hygiene factors are those factors which when adequate or reasonable in a job, make employee to do more and think creatively and do not make them dissatisfied. These factors are extrinsic to work. Hygiene factors can lead to dissatisfaction of employees and decrease creativity if not available.

To avoid any negative impact on the employees the leader must understand that hygiene factors are required to avoid dissatisfaction and ideas generation. This is because they help define the job environment. They symbolized the physiological needs which the individuals wanted and expected to be fulfilled. Hygiene factors include; pay policy, relationship, salary and working condition. To get rid of these hygiene factors you must be ready to

- fix poor and obstructive company policies;
- provide effective, supportive, and nonintrusive supervision;
- create and support a culture of respect and dignity for all team employees;
- ensure that wages are competitive;
- build job status by providing meaningful work for all positions; and
- provide job security.

On the other hand, motivational factors could be defined as those needed for the actual job performance. Motivational factors yield positive satisfaction. These factors are inherent to work and motivate the employees for a superior performance. These factors are called satisfiers and are involved in performing the job.

Employees find these factors intrinsically rewarding. The motivators symbolized the psychological needs that were perceived as an additional benefit. Motivational factors include recognition, empowerment, responsibility, inclusion, growth opportunity, and association with others. All these factors help with innovation and creativity as they help improve employees' sense of belonging and self-fulfillment. They feel like they are part of the larger system when these factors are present and provided to them.

Things to consider when looking for motivational factors include
- providing opportunities for achievement;
- recognizing workers' contributions;
- creating work that is rewarding and matches the skills and abilities of the worker;
- giving as much responsibility to each team member as possible;
- providing opportunities to advance in the company through internal promotions; and
- offering internal training and development opportunities so people can pursue positions they want.

Creativity

Promoting creativity in the organization will require the leader to have a clear understanding of leadership skills and competencies that are essential for knowledge workers to see and feel as they help promote their ability to be involved. You need more knowledge workers with creative minds if you want to be relevant in your industry as an organization, you need them for new ideas and new thinking, which are foundation for innovation and growth. When a knowledge worker perceives that his or her job requirements are meaningful and personally important, he or she will spend more efforts on understanding a problem from multiple perspectives, searching for a solution using a wide variety of information from multiple sources, and generating a significant number of alternatives by connecting diverse sources of information to create new ideas and solutions.

Your job is to make sure you have a solid internal structure, better leadership, and standards that can promote critical thinking and ideas. At the same time, as a leader, the need for encouragement and recognition should not be excluded. It's important for you to help create external factors that will speak to individual internal factors, which will in turn help generate new energy for new ideas.

The leader must know how to promote employees' needs for curiosity and activity. By giving them the opportunity to find challenging problems, solve them, and implement their own solutions, it will influence the way they think, associate with, and relate to each other, which will eventually influence their creative ability as a team. We know that work accomplishments are the best way to motivate knowledge workers, as this helps with their sense of belonging and self-esteem.

Another thing that is important for you to strive for when trying to promote creativity is teamwork, which goes over well in a creative environment because it helps promote knowledge sharing and integration of employees' ideas and processes. Effective teamwork promotes better interaction and relationships, which is needed for bonding and dependability. New ideas are shared through meaningful and constructive dialogue because of the existence of strong ties among employees. These strong ties often produce new skills, ideas, and innovations the organization needs for competitiveness.

You can engage in the following areas when trying to promote creativity in the organization: perhaps offer workshops, seminars, corporate retreats, and celebratory gatherings.

It must be understood that creativity among employees and in the organization as a whole is a continuous behavior of finding problems and finding creative means of solving these problems. Creativity can also mean finding new ways to improve existing products, services, procedures, and processes. It can also be how to improve and sustain the satisfaction and well-being of organizational employees. For this to happen you must help develop an environment or climate where creative ideas are likely to emerge. You must encourage, promote, and enhance behaviors that will stimulate employees to develop new ideas. You must be flexible in your approach, which includes dealing with shortcomings and failures. You must display confidence and be a no-blame manager when mistakes are made or when new ideas are not working out as planned.

Remember, your employees are looking for your leadership, and they will be scrutinizing you as you interact with them. You must strive to be a role model at all times as this will help with their perception of your support for creativity and innovation.

As you establish these things, it's important for you to not forget the relative impact of your relationship with employees. In my book *Healthcare Management: Are Social Skills the Answer?* (2007), I talked about the three C concepts of managing an organization. These are confident, caring, and comfort. When your employees see you showing a caring attitude toward their well-being, their confident level increases, which also influences their performance level; which eventually makes the organization a better place to work. An encouraging working environment that is combined with an inspiring personal relationship has the tendency to produce more creative minds and ideas. Your day to day activities must support creative ideas and promote relevant tasks that can promote employee's creativity. A leader who is open and listens to employees will have a better chance of creating an innovative workforce. It's important that your employees know where you stand on every new project as this will help remove any doubt or discourage confusion and discouragement. You must make sure you communicate an attractive and realistic vision of what they can accomplish by being creative.

The leader must not forget the power in team-working environments. Try to capitalize on the current positive working environment by promoting brainstorming and dialogue. Brainstorming can be used to generate new ideas and can be done by encouraging participation in decision-making, seeking their input, organizing events, and opening them to new ideas they're unfamiliar with. You can use this to promote team building and cohesion. Employees should be encouraged to bring their new ideas and write them down for others to debate and discuss. Through brainstorming, better ideas can be developed because this method allows for debate and criticisms. Employees are able to say what they think about the new ideas.

We know that when employees are able to discuss issues, they are more likely to bring out new ideas and solutions. Also, because of their involvement in idea generation, they are likely to take risks, explore ideas, and be playful with ideas.

Promoting creativity also means you're using your position in the organization to promote employee engagement. Employees are looking for a creative working environment. Your consistent behavior can prime employees' attention and facilitate their efforts toward creativity. I learned long ago that when people know how importance and significant creativity is to their works, they have the tendency to be more creative. This shows you that you must not relent in your efforts of letting them know how important they are to the growth of the company and that their contributions are valued and respected. You need to clearly state the company's mission at all times, because this can enable a greater focus on new idea development and subsequent successful innovation.

In her work on creativity, Amabile (1997) listed the following attributes as areas that must be considered by managers when looking to be more creative:

- management education (types of motivation, their sources, their effects on performance, and their susceptibility to various work environments) should be improved
- external motivators and the context in which they are presented
- development of strong orientation toward innovation, which is clearly communicated and enacted from highest levels of management throughout the organization

- organization must orient itself toward the generation, communication, careful consideration, and development of new ideas, non-controlling reward and recognition for creative work, mechanism for developing new ideas, and an active flow of ideas
- work groups should be constituted of diversely skilled individuals with a shared motivation for their work and a willingness to share and constructively criticize each other's ideas
- employees should be given adequate resources to carry out their work and sufficient time to consider alternative approaches

Examine these steps and come up with your own template on how you can improve engagement, creativity, and new ideas. Don't forget, the organization is depending on you to help with this endeavor, which means the survival of the organization depends on your ability to promote and encourage idea generation that can influence innovation.

Great organization can be possible when employees are allowed to use their knowledge and creativity. Honestly, your organization needs to be innovative, as this will allow it to build its operation around its consumers more effectively and wisely. Doing this can generate a solid customer base, give a better profit margin, and maintain loyal partners.

Points to Remember

- Two heads are mostly better than one.
- With the right environment and encouragement we can all succeed.
- Use your position to enlist those with potential.
- You were not hired to do it alone, you were hired to help build a community of learners and doers.

Chapter 9
Be a Focused Change Agent

One purpose for this book is to help shed light on basic management principles that can help a growing manager be a successful leader and breathe new life into an existing one.

Fear of Change

Change is needed and should be about the future of the organization. Leaders are known as agent of change, which means they must always look to the future and help prepare the organization for these changes. Changes come with fear— fear of the unknown and of failure. The job of the leader is to help defuse some of these fears. There will be resistance to change because of unknown factors. The leader should not hesitate to use his or her influence to communicate the need for change.

There cannot be any significant change in the life of the organization when there is no new focus or change in standards and operation. According to Aristotle, "We are what we repeatedly do. Excellence, therefore, is not an act but a habit."

The call for change is growing; the only way to survive it is to look for opportunities that the environment is providing. According to Maxwell (2012), "No matter what you have gone through in your life or what you are currently going through, you have the opportunity in the midst of the pain, but it's there. You must be willing to not only look for it but pursue it."

The ideas you're looking for already exist, therefore, you can help your organization look for them. American academic and politician Paul Wellstone said, "The future will belong to those who have passion and to those who are willing to make the personal commitment to make organization better." This means as a leader, developing change will be a key role that you will have to work with because this is the only way your organization can have a sustainable long-term organizational performance in an unstable, unpredictable, and inflexible environment. You must see change as an engaging, energetic, and equitable process that involves political, emotional, and behavioral realities.

You must be willing to deal with the complex nature of change and all the key players that will be engaged during the change processes.

It's also the expectation that you will have a clear understanding of how and why changes are often difficult to achieve. You must know that within your organization, employees have unique ideas and opinions about how the company should be managed. They have fears and attitudes that may impact the change itself if not well managed.

According to Vakola and Nikolaou (2005), "Attitudes toward change in general consist of a person's cognitions about change, affective reactions to change, and behavioral tendency toward change." This means change can be received with excitement and happiness or anger and fear while employees' response to it may range from positive intentions to support the change to negative intentions to oppose it.

Before introducing any change, the leader must know that having a positively charged working environment will be crucial for successful and effective change. Therefore, it's your responsibility to let your employees observe socially supportive behavior from you, because any lack of a supportive environment can produce or enhance deeply negative attitudes.

Your employees want to see that you have passion for change, that you have the courage to initiate change, and that you have the vision for change, because this will assist you on how you handle the environment's complexity. Through your commitment, drive, and time, your employees should have no doubt about your call for a new change either in behavior or in practice. You should effectively help manage change by fostering a climate that will be conducive for the planned change.

The Three Functions of Change

These three functions of a manager—controlling, influencing, and staffing— are crucial during change. You must know how to use your influence to galvanize support from your superiors because without their support, it will be highly difficult to institute any meaningful changes. Also, it's expected that you will use your influencing function to solicit and secure a long-lasting commitment for the change from your employees. You must have a clear understanding of change before introducing it to your employees.

According to business management expert Tom Peters, "To meet the demands of the fast-changing competitive scene, we must simply learn to love change as much as we have hated it in the past."

It must be realized that when change is introduced, there is always fear and a sense of intimidation from employees. Your function should help reduce and eliminate some of these fears. You should know that any new change brings increased workload to employees, so you must know how to help them adapt to new ways of working and behaving. Resources are as important as the support that you are providing to them, which means you must make sure there are enough resources, staffing, and any other things that may contribute to the smooth transition and implementation of the change. These are necessary before any meaningful change can take place. There must be a sufficient infrastructure in place that will help with the training, learning, and knowledge sharing among employees, which can help improve the chances for a successful adoption of the change.

It's crucial to know how to use organization's strategy tools to define the purpose, reason, and urgency for the planned change, as well as potential benefits and risks as a result of the change. You should also know how you're going to use the organizational structure to your advantage during the change implementation. When you have a clear knowledge of the mission and the internal structure of the company, you will have the right people on your side, and they can help in the communication of the intended changes, which can help gain more support and buy-in from employees.

It's important for you to be available at all time, because as their manager, you will be their first port of call, and you will need to know how to help resolve and reassure them with their questions, worries, and concerns. The reason for this is that the change capacity depends upon organizational employees who are knowledgeable about the change. If they don't understand what's going on, the probability of not having meaningful and effective changes will be higher than expected.

The manager has to become a change agent and a creator. Inspirational leaders often rely heavily on their instincts to know when to advocate for a new direction or a difference in operational behavior. A change agent will constantly ask employees to play a more substantive and direct role in the creation of a better organization and a solid customer base that can be used to promote the company's vision and mission. As a leader you will become a change agent because of your knowledge, experience, and history. You will be asked to be responsible for leading change. Based on your position, educational and professional preparation, and your experience in the use of change tools, the expectations will be for you to help the organization initiate and coordinate change.

Key Tools for Change

- Be visionary about the future.
- Ensure adequate resources.
- Stay motivated about the process and the expected positive outcomes.
- Be inspirational.

Another thing you must understand before you bring about the change is the resistance that can result. Resistance occurs due to change having the tendency to disrupt the status quo. Therefore, what is needed from you is to support them and have a clear understanding for these behaviors. You must demonstrate a positive attitude toward any resistance. It must be understood that resistance to change is a byproduct of emotional reactions and behaviors that have to do with the feeling of losing control and power that the employees gained over the years. To avoid resistance, you must practice participative leadership, which mean more and more of your employees will be involved in the designing and implementing of the new idea.

You should always anticipate change as a manager. It's the only thing that is going to happen, so you must learn how to listen and learn about the industry, the organization, and the people inside and out. You should communicate this to your employees when you know it's probable and let them know the nature of the change, why the change will occur, and if the change is going to have any effect on the organization's strategic direction.

When doing your organizational assessment and looking for able and capable people to help in the formation and creation of change, you must know that at all times you have four different types of employees or groups in your organization and community, and what is required of you is knowing how you deal with each group. You have

The early adopters, who are ready to go with you and your plan for change. They are passionate and enthusiastic about the change. They know that without change, the organization will lose its competitive edge and relevance. They are ready to commit to change and ready to spend time and knowledge toward a better organization

The late adopters are not willing to accept your idea at the initial stage. They like to take their time to review, digest, and study before they get on board. They often have positive attitudes toward the change and are optimistic about the future. They like to watch for early commitment and dedication from employees and, most importantly, from their leaders.

The doubting Thomases and the fence sitters are employees who retain the memory of what happened before. They have seen changes come and go and have become used to it. They are cynical about any changes because of their experiences. They're not willing to commit their time or energy because they witnessed too much change failure, with too many promises not being met. The only way they will join your team is when they see proof of change and the truthfulness of their leaders.

"Stone heads" or resistors are fighters against change, and their role (as they see it) is to fight from beginning to end. They always look for like-minded people by coming up with strange and untenable excuses for not committing to change. They have their own reasons for their negativity. It may be fear of the unknown, past experiences, or their own selfish interests. Your job is not to spend too much time on these people because of the time and energy that it would take to convince them to embrace the change. If at all possible, you want to see if they can be converted and change to become fence sitters.

Factors that must be considered and entrenched in your daily operations as you begin to work on a change process in the organization include

- Communication: It's important for you as a leader to think about you want say and how you want to say it before you go out to communicate the needs change. Your communication skills can help in the reinforcement of your id and serve as motivation for some employees.
- Listening: For your change to be effective, you need to make sure to hone y listening skills. Listening should be about understanding, not persuading. The goal should be to understand how your employees feel about the change. Listening can help you gain new insights into planning for the change.
- Feedback: Change will call for feedback from both sides of the equation. leaders must learn how to provide feedback to employees and employ provide feedback to their leaders. It should be a learning experience everyone. To gain more employee interest for this change, let your feedback contain the right information, and focus on the major strengths of employ and areas that you observed for improvement. To continue to retain and at more positive employees into your team, your feedback during change must positive and clear. You need to learn how to identify one good thing that happened during the change or was done by the employees. It should specify about what impact it had on the overall objective.
- Building trust: for change to happen and be successful, it's important to know how to build a trusting relationship with your employees. They must have trusting view about the change and what it will mean for the organization. presence of trust can enhance your efforts to fulfill your mission on changes. Because your words and actions help set the tone, you must maintain a c face at all times. Learn how to respond to concerns and questions that employee may bring to you. When you take your time and summon your

courage address their concerns you are directly building trust around the change. Refr from seen punishments as the last correctional step when mistakes are ma Every accomplishments and success should be followed by a thank you. them know their efforts are appreciated.

- Create an internal structure that will help support the change. The inter structure examines relationships, communications, and collaborations between employees. The culture must be ready for the change as well. You can con the change you are creating by modeling the behavior, role playing behavior, and verbalizing your support for the behavior. The leader must consistent in his message; there should be no second thoughts or confusion messages about the change. Openness and transparency will go a long way the implementation of change.

Points to Remember

- Learn how to adapt your leadership style when introducing change into the organization.
- Learn how to create a shared vision for your change by involving all major shareholders in the change process.
- If at all possible use teams for your change as many heads are better than one.
- Learn how to foster employee buy-in through empowerment and collaborative leadership styles.
- Learn how to use communication to gain understanding.
- Learn how to use feedback and listening to improve employee satisfaction and to identify opportunities for improvement.

Chapter 10
The Power of a Moral and Ethical Leader

We will now look at ethical leaders. According to Trevino et al. (2000), ethical leaders are fair, principled decision-makers and behave ethically in their daily lives. Ethical leadership can be defined as "the demonstration of normatively conduct behavior through personal actions and interpersonal relationships" (Brown, Trevino, and Harrison 2005). The overall assumption is that ethical leadership behavior will help reduce employee anxiety by being polite, considerate, open, trustworthy, and honest. The role of a growing leader is to help stress the importance of sticking to high ethical conduct to employees and to the organization's customers and partners.

In being conscious ethically and morally, this means you as the leader understand that character and integrity do serve as the cornerstone for your success and that of the organization, and having an ethical culture in place will help increase production, decrease staff turnover, and attract loyal customers. The overall objective for any morally courageous leader is to help create a culture that is consistent with the organization's values and standards. At the same time, the organization is looking for your help in creating an environment that is honest, just, and always in the best interests of those that you lead and serve. The expectation is that you will always display the highest moral behavior and that you will help in the provision of a moral framework that can be used to create the expected moral values for the organization.

One of those is the ethical behavior of the leader. Leaders are to inspire and persuade others to act for the common goals and objectives that represent the values, wants, needs, and aspirations of themselves and the people they're managing and leading. Through moral and ethical behavior, a better organization is possible. It's a fact that for any organization to grow and be relevant to both its employees and customers there must be a common belief in ethical and moral behaviors.

As a growing leader you should understand that the final outcome for an ethical and morally oriented organization are good customer loyalty, more committed and satisfied employees, and more efficient service delivery and can lead to increased market share for the organization. In every action and step taken by the leader, others are looking, and what you do can have a huge impact on their moral thinking and acceptance. Your behavior can influence employees' perception of engagement and organizational justice because a leader's unethical behaviors have been attributed to some of the unethical behaviors that are seen in most organizations.

The growing leader has to find ways to help foster an ethical culture for the organization. It must stimulate employees' well-being and their commitment to organizational goals and their willingness to report wrongdoing in the organization. You are to help set a clear and high ethical standard for employees by engaging in open and honest communications at all times and frequently discuss ethics and make it a salient part of the organization. It's also expected that you will help shape ethical conduct and perceived justice at all levels. You must remember that when behaviors are seen as ethical, it can help influence the decision-making and behaviors of employees, which can have a positive influence on their work habits and ethics and result in better overall results. Your functions on ethical image creation will also be seen from how you are able to help translate organization's mission, vision, and values statements into a set of shared values and a moral compass for every employee.

To be able to carry out these expectations successfully, you must engage in the following behaviors:
- Engage in open communication and be clear on your expectations concerning the ethical conduct of your employees.
- Let your behavior be in line with expectations.
- Make ethical resources available for your employees and be supportive; this is an indication of how you and the organization are encouraging ethical behaviors.
- Promote transparency at all levels. Awareness of the consequences of one's action can help discourage any unethical behavior.
- Promote open dialogue and allow employees to discuss their concerns and problems on any ethical issues they might have.
- Learn how to hold employees accountable for any unethical behaviors. Have a robust reward system in place for those employees who demonstrate the ethical behaviors and values that are promoted by the organization.
- Be ready to set good example. Display the highest moral standards and ethical conduct in everyday talk, actions, decisions, and behaviors.
- Practice participative leadership style by empowering, motivating, and engaging in character building of employees.
- Be willing to treat employees fairly by trusting them and listening to their concerns.
- Help in the development of organizational practices, policies, and procedures on ethical standards.
- Use every encounter with employees to communicate that they are doing the right thing as expected, encouraged, and valued by leadership.
- Embody positive personal characteristics and seek to

influence employees by actively managing ethical conduct.

A template on ethical behaviors and expectations can help you on your journey and in your efforts to create an ethical culture. When discussing ethical behavior, it's important to acknowledge the difference between ethics and morals. Generally speaking, ethics is a course of study about a culture's philosophy on standards and conduct. Morals, on the other hand, are the practice of the ethics of a culture—in other words, their behavioral norms and customs.

You should always have at the back of your mind that your employees will not engage in any unethical behavior when their leaders treat them fairly and have the belief that their leaders' behaviors are good for the organization. Your ethical culture should emphasize which behaviors are allowed and which are prohibited.

The key element in ethical culture is known as organizational justice, which is the foundation on which ethical and moral leadership is based. The table below will provide the three features of organizational justice as defined by Colquitt, Noe, and Jackson (2002), and how you as the leader should adjust your leadership style to recognize each step and help in the creation of a healthy working environment. The people you are leading should feel comfortable with you and know that most of your actions and decisions will be equitable. They should not have to second guess your decisions and actions; they should know you by your words and know that your words and actions are reliable. It's important for your behavior to mimic your communication, which means what you say and do should not vary in meaning and interpretation.

Organizational Justice and Ethical Leader Framework

Perceived Distributional Justice	Perceived Procedural Justice	Perceived Interactional Justice
Based on Fairness	Perceived Fairness	Perceived Information Accuracy
Actions and decisions are considered fair if based on rules that are acknowledged as just	In decision-making, benefits allocation distribution of resources.	Consider or recognize the viewpoints of subordinates. Subordinates believe decisionmakers should be neutral and free of any personal interests
The allocation of resources is done based on the needs and contributions of employees	There is a consistency, bias suppression, accuracy, and ethicality	The report should contain the explanation for the decision and the reason for its acceptance
The manager has used the fairness principle to allocate, determine, and reward each employee based on the fairness principle	The rules are applied the same way to all employees. Procedures are considered fair if a similar procedure brings about similar results	The decision-makers should be neutral and free of any personal interest, focusing only on the fairness of the procedure

Points to Remember

- Growing leaders should not neglect employees; everything should be done to support their well-being.
- Growing leaders have to know the benefits and advantages of fairness. You should treat every employee fairly.
- Growing leaders must empower and discover employees' hidden talents, which are needed for a ethical working environment.
- Growing leaders must not deviate from moral and ethical principles.
- Growing leaders should have a clear understanding of his ethical and unethical behaviors on employees and the

organization.
- Growing leaders should encourage open communication on various ethical issues.
- Growing leaders must understand the hidden signs of unethical behavior.
- Growing leaders should see value in the organization's vision and mission statement and use them to create long-lasting pillars for an ethical culture.
- Growing leaders should make sure his or her behaviors and actions inspire employees to cultivate ethical and moral behaviors at all times.
- Growing leaders should know when to step forward and take responsibility for all major management decisions and actions.
- Growing leaders should have a clear understanding that the only reason for behavior is the thoughts, which means you should always evaluate the costs and benefits of each behavior and the influence each can have on the organization and its people.
- Growing leaders should help develop behavioral modification self-awareness skills on ethics and assist employees on how to recognize and identify the consequences of their lack of ethical and moral behaviors on the organization and its employees.
- Growing leaders should know that failure of character is the most important reason leaders fail in leadership.
- Growing leaders must understand the power of honesty and what influence it can have on leader-employee relationships.

Improved employee participation is always possible when employees see that their leader is honest, transparent, and truthful at all times.

Chapter 11
Be an Engaging Leader

In managing today's complex and sophisticated working environments, a manager must know how to involve the entire community in whatever programs or events that might be going on in the organization. A successful leader understands that "it takes a village." In making the organization great and profitable, it will take the entire community to be engaged and involved. The leader must know that two heads are often better than one when it comes to leadership. Through your leadership style and approach, you should continue to increase the level of engagement from all groups of stakeholders. An engaged employee fully understands what his or her roles are and who is fully involved in all available activities both within and outside the organization. This individual is enthusiastic about his or her work, wants to contribute, and is willing to go that extra mile for the sake of the common goal.

Employee engagement in organizations is a product of working environments and any other motivational factors that the organization has put in place. The objective for engaging employees is about how the organization is going to do well and be more productive with good financial standing.

As a leader, your goal should not be to only communicate the goals and objectives of the organization and not just inform employees of its vision. You should know how to engage employees and empower them to be useful in the organization. People are always happy when they are asked to be part of something good, something meaningful and important. You should have a mechanism on how to tap into their pockets of reserve for more and better ideas.

Engaging employees can have the following impacts on the organization and its overall outlook:
- They help drive results.
- They help make a difference.
- They help promote strong working relationships.
- They create positive and effective cultures.
- They help recruit and retain employees by attracting knowledge workers to organization.
- They help promote ownership and loyalty of other employees in organization, which may turn into high productivity and performance.

How many times have you heard people, especially employees, say, "I like the way he came down to talk to us," or "He has just demonstrated that he cares about the little people," or "Coming down to talk to us and listen to us and feel for what we are going through meant a lot to me and my team."

Level of engagement is about empowering, collaboration, and respect for others' feelings and concerns. Every leader must know that everything we do depends on the successful transfer of meaning from one group to another. Your relationship should not be for one group, it should be for all groups.

A leader's ability and willingness to seek constructive and meaningful relationships with the population often leads to new conversations. Every interaction you have should stimulate rich conversations, exchanges of ideas, and utilization of new principles. In creating this relationship, it's important to make sure that your position and title do not drive how you interact with people. Your relationship should come from live interactions with employees, attending staff meetings, and organizing focus groups and town hall meetings.

Another thing you can do to foster this relationship is by modeling behaviors that promote trust in the minds of the employees. I have worked with a leader who enjoyed having staff in his office for meetings. This leader believed it was not enough for him to meet employees at their work place; they needed to come to him in his workplace, which happened to be his office. This type of behavior helps reinforce confidence, beliefs, and trust in the minds of employees.

Engagement Example

I'd like to use the 2015 NBA final game between the Cleveland Cavaliers and Golden State Warriors as an example. In this game, there were two starters that every basketball fan was watching to see how they would perform. On the Cavaliers side was LeBron James, and on the Warriors side was Stephen Curry. Both played well for their team and demonstrated leadership behaviors that allowed their teammates to excel. I will focus on LeBron James because of the way he carried his teammates with him despite adversity. The team was missing two of its key players for this final series, which made it difficult to sustain the tempo and tenacity the team is known for.

What was witnessed by all was an outstanding performance by the Cavaliers that has been ruled out by most of having what was needed to face the most balanced and talented Warrior team. When talking about engagement and what leaders' ability to engage team members can do on the overall performance of the team or organization could be seen from the way LeBron James engaged his teammates. Recognizing that he would not be able to carry the team to the end, he came out strong by engaging the rest of the team. By doing this, we were all surprised to see how active, engaged, and motivated the rest of the team were during the series. The fans got to know more about the team members and their potential. By engaging others to be part of history, LeBron helped bring out his teammates' potentials that fans did not know about. Because of this high level of engagement, we saw how the tables were turned and they were able to win some games and the final series. This unique performance by the Cleveland Cavaliers supports the general assumption in management that says 80 percent of the innovation and improvement ideas often come from frontline staff and not from the manager/leader. This was so in the Cavaliers' case because each understood what had to be done. They had an idea and knew what need to get done to get teammates engage and ready for the final series.

This is also true with your team. When you take the time to find out more about them and their styles, needs, and wants, your probability of increasing their level of engagement will be higher than expected. This is because your employees are closest to the process, often closest to the customers and their needs. They see the problem and often have the solution. Take time to make them part of the process and it shall produce the result you are looking for.

Promoting Engagement

When you attend any leadership training, the presenters often tell you that a good leader values employees and their well-being, successes, and achievements. These cannot happen if the employees do not trust and have confidence in their boss, or if they have not been engaged and asked to be part of the solutions. Engaged employees are motivated and dedicated to the overall goals of the organization.

- Have a clear direction and goals for employees to look forward to because when there are no clear goals and directions, it's likely the employees will have nothing to look to and be engaged in their daily assignments and work.
- Let your behavior and attitudes reflect the organizational vision.

- Be present at all times, because a leader who is visible will be able to help in the creation of a better culture for the organization.
- Enhance engagement with better communication and transparency. It's important that you tell your employees what's going on in the organization, and let them know their expectations and how they can be involved.
- Promote conflict resolution among employees. A one-sided conflict resolution can result in unhappy employees and can deprive them of being engaged in the organization. It's equally important for the leader to promote healthy conflict. Failure to address conflicts in a way that brings positive results can lead to unhappiness and decrease level of engagement.
- Be consistent and dependable in your dealings with employees at all time.
- Work to attain meaningful career development for your employees. Challenge them when the opportunity presents itself. Seek input from your employees regarding their career goals. Let them know you are interested in their professional growth and development.
- Find time to celebrate with and congratulate your employees for significant accomplishments or contributions. Your feedback should not be only when they do something wrong or when they fail to achieve as expected. You should let them know how they are doing at regular intervals.
- As previously mentioned, collaboration and inclusion foster employee morale and trust. But they also promote engagement. Make sure you collaborate with your employees; let them know their input is needed. Include them in decision-making processes as this helps with ego and sense of belonging.

Points to Remember

- Employee engagement not only drives productivity, it helps with culture creation.
- Employee engagement helps promote a variety of outcomes that are good for employees and customers.
- Engagement enhances pride and sense of belonging of employees.
- Use your culture and your people to create an engaging work environment.
- Know when there is a change in the level of engagement of employees and make necessary adjustments that can help sustain engagement.
- Note that engagement is a win-win for employees and the organization.

Chapter 12
Building Strategic Direction

In assuming the role of a leader or manager, it's important to have a plan on how to help contribute to the growth and development of your organization. One way is by thinking strategically at all times. The need to understand the internal and external environment is highly essential for any successful manager. It's a requirement to maintain an ongoing assessment of the environment and be able to evaluate those developments that may interfere with operations. As a leader, your continuous monitoring and analyzing signals from the environment will help with your plans on how to react and approach each signal and ensure the organization is ready for these new demands.

In your role, it's important to view the relationship between your organization and the environment as a two-way street, which means you're not only going to be focusing on how to react to the environment and its signals, you'll be thinking about how to positively influence the environment. You must pay attention to your employees and customers. They must play significant roles in the overall strategic plan; therefore, they must be involved in the creation and implementation of a strategic direction that is meaningful and measurable for the organization.

Apart from helping with the creation of meaningful dialog and understanding the strategic direction of the organization, you're the only one who can judge whether the existing strategic direction is working or if there's a need for new direction. Because of this your involvement in the strategic planning should help in providing value, improve the quality of strategic decisions, and generate a sense of ownership and identification with organizational goals and objectives. What is required of you is a deep personal commitment coupled with the ability to help align employees with a vision. You can help with this alignment by challenging long-held assumptions, seeking new pathways for learning, and preparing the organization to promote creativity and participation.

In your efforts on strategic development, you will be required to help the organization sell its vision. You must know that visions are powerless and ineffective unless they are derived, shared, bought and embraced by your employees and individuals, who will collectively achieve them. You will be required to lead by fostering a shared vision for the organization through a collaborative and democratic leadership style. Your leadership style should challenge your employees to be creative and have a common goal for the future. The future of the organization will depend on how employees see the vision and its implications on their future. The vision can only become a living force for change only when you and your employees actually believe that it can be used to shape how the future will look either for the organization or for the individual.

Hostile Workplaces

The ultimate goal is to have an environment that fosters teamwork, collaboration, inclusion, and creativity as they are the likely variables that can help encourage participation of employees in the strategic plan. It's important for you to help create an environment that will allow your employees to experience the peace that is in human nature, which enhances friendliness and happiness of employees. This type of environment is known as a positive and encouraging work environment. In an environment that is perceived as hostile by employees, it will be difficult for the manager to have followers for the strategic direction and plan. Hostile environment often result into disruptive information processing which makes information sharing and communication difficult. The hostile environment can elevate employees' anxiety level about their future and the future of the organization. The perception of employees in an environment that is toxic and hostile often allows for wrong processing and utilization, which may result in wrong strategic directions for the organization.

You must help prevent tension because of its impact on anxiety. Tension has promotes anxiety and defensiveness. The tendency to make a wrong decision in an anxious situation is high. Strategic decision-making in hostile working environments can impede growth and influence the experience and perceptions of employees. Hostile work environments can create unnecessary fear in the mind of the employees, and fear of failure can paralyze decision-making and inhibit engagement and creativity, which can have adverse effects on the direction of the organization.

To promote employees' involvement in strategic thinking, you must help reduce tension, decrease anxiety, and promote opportunities for open dialogue, staff participation, and two-ways communication and make sure they have the tools and resources to succeed in their tasks and roles. Your management support and involvement will be crucial to the final strategic plan and should promote confidence in themselves and the organization. The support you provide should reinforce confidence in the organization, help promote trust, and enhance a risk-taking behavior that can help with creative thinking and a sense of belonging.

Communicating the Strategy

Another great thing that can help you with your strategic plan with your employees is to constantly talk and communicate reasons for the strategic plan and make sure you are linking your communication to the vision and mission. Communicating the vision to them will help challenge them to create creatively; it will allow them to have a clear understanding of what the future plan is and what needs to happen before this great and encouraging future can be achieved. The only way you will be able to advance your strategic thinking among your team/employees is to learn how to effectively share information with your employees. The communication speed and accuracy can influence how employees react to the information that is being shared with them. Your employees must not feel as if they are not part of the team or not wanted during the strategic planning. All employees must be respected, valued and included in the draft of the future plans for the organization. You should your communication to seek feedback and clarification from your employees. You need to learn from them whether they understand your future plan, and if there is anything that has to be changed or re-structured. Let your communication be upward in nature because of its advantages. Upward communication makes it easier for your employees to ask questions, to express their concerns, and to provide you with feedback on areas of interest.

In looking at the future, it's important for you to know how to share results and celebrate achievements with employees. Employees who understand performance data can contribute meaningfully and constructively in the future direction of the company. Performance data should be used to drive the strategic future. Sharing this data with employees can enable them to help you in making correct and effective strategic decision and can allow them to have an inside look at what can be improved and corrected. Their successes must be celebrated as this can help promote engagement, loyalty to the course, and belief in the organization's future.

The most important thing for the leader to do is promote innovation and creativity of employees. Innovation can only be possible when the leader understands the power of communication, behavior, and support. Your employees must see that your behavior and communication are aligned with each other. What you are saying or asking your employees to do must reflect in your behaviors and interactions. You should not engage in deceit.

I worked for an organization where the top man could not be trusted. What this leader said and did were completely different from each other. There was a time when he told us about hiring practices and what the organization would be looking for from leaders and managers. We were told the management style would not tolerate discrimination, injustice, and favoritism. Unfortunately, what actually happened to most minority employees in this organization was opposite of what this leader said. Most minority employees were removed, fired, or demoted, and this leader was aware of this behavior but promoted it. He lied to the employees, the community, and to employees of the political representatives.

This type of communication and behavior as demonstrated by this leader cannot promote innovation. As a matter of fact, his unspoken behavior set this organization back; there was no trust from the employees.

To promote innovation that will help set the organization to the perfect future of creativity and productivity, the leader must learn how to surround himself with good people, with experts and truthful people. The leader must not just surround himself with people who are ready to tell him or her what the leader wants to hear. This type of behavior promotes lying, fearfulness, and a poor work environment.

It's a fact that leading in today's health care environment will demand flexibility, a high degree of tolerance, and a super competency portfolio from the leaders. Most working environments are ever-changing, which means the leader/manager must have a clear understanding of his or her role.

In order to be seen as an effective leader, there are some basic functions that can help propel the organization to a higher level if they are done well. These functions, according to Dunn and Haimann (2015), are influencing, financing, staffing, controlling, and planning. To be able to fulfill any of these functions effectively, the manager must have the understanding of what staff engagement and participation would mean to innovation, and also contribute to the overall performance of the organization. These five functions should be used to create and foster a creative and performing culture. A performing culture makes entrance and exit to be less difficult and more interesting. In a performing culture the relationship is therapeutic and so also is the communication. The change that is happening in industries, calls for a creative leadership strength and skills with high moral and ethical standards. Creating a sound culture can provide a solid foundation for the organization and this can be used to promote and enhance behaviors that are going to be beneficial to the entire organization. It's important for managers to understand how to identify, recognize, and sustain happy stakeholders.

Looking at a leader's functions, as described by Dunn and Haimann (2015), the most important and crucial function among managers is influence. The expectations of every organization are for managers/leaders to use their position to help influence employees toward goals and objectives of the organization. Managers' effectiveness will be based on several measurements, some on how the manager can create and nurture a thriving work environment, which fosters team building, relationships, understanding, respect, inclusion, and communication. It's an environment that will help with innovation and creativity. The ability of the manager to create and sustain this environment will depend on leadership style, background, perceptions of the job, and position.

Understandably, effectiveness of any leader/manager is not a sole product of the leadership styles; it's a combination of other things, as discovered by Fiedler et al. (2012). Other mitigating factors on their work on contingency theory are situation and the personality of the leader/manager. The type of leadership style the leader uses will depend on the situation and its nature. This is because situations are not the same in scope and in severity, which means each one of them will be unique and require different leadership styles. The way a charismatic, democratic and servant leader will approach problems will be different from how an authoritarian and dictatorship leader will manage the problem. In the overall analysis, strategic direction will depend on the leader, the leadership style, and communication and behavior.

The need for sound organizational principles will be paramount to the success of the organization regardless of the people and services that are being offered. The leader must engage in behaviors that are likely to produce good and lasting results on the organization. Because of the need for high-quality products, excellent service delivery, and the increase in the demands by all major stakeholders, it will be beneficial and advantageous for the organization to have employees who are dedicated and always ready to perform and help the organization beyond expectations. This type of performance can only happen when there is a leader who is compassionate and caring and knows how to motivate employees.

In his work on motivation, Barbuto (2005) portrayed leaders as sources of motivation. They concluded that the behaviors executed by a leader must be captivating enough to ensure its followership.

Miner (2005) wrote, "The more leaders execute charismatic behaviors, the more its followers will demonstrate organizational citizenship behaviors and feeling of meaningfulness in work and lives increases."

When describing how a leader can get more from their employees, Bass (1997) wrote, "Leaders can acquire the best performance from their followers through building relationships with them." When looking at leadership styles, and how to use leadership styles to get more from employees, Bass was of the opinion that a leader who understands and embraces the transformational style of leadership should have no problem getting employees to be more productive and innovative because a transformational leadership is characterized by actions and behaviors that are above and beyond the employment contract. A transformational leader is known for the attentiveness to a combination of feelings, independence, and empowerment, which satisfy employees' needs of sell-autonomy."

For a manager to create an environment that promotes a positive work environment that will be useful for innovation and better strategic planning for the organization, he or she must embrace the transformational and participative leadership styles. This is because if used successfully, both styles can produce this type of environment. The transformational leadership style can produce long-lasting advantages on the organization; it can help with transparency and communication. The transformational leadership style can lead to high-quality care delivery, better and improved work habits, and the creation of a better perception on psychological safety by employees. The organizational climate is always better with these two leadership styles. Employees are open; they feel involved and engaged. Because of the open communication style of a transformational leader, the interpersonal relationship between the leader and the employees is improved.

Points to Remember

- Create a vision and communicate the vision to employees.
- Seek support for the vision.

- Ensure that your communication and behavior are saying the same thing.
- Practice open and transparent leadership style.
- Include all in the planning.
- Seek potential knowledge workers when trying to create the future for the organization together.
- Encourage and promote innovation.
- Practice participative leadership.
- Let your strategic plan reflects your values and leadership style.
- Discourage closed-door planning; make it open to all.
- Take time to learn the culture and seek help from others, don't be a know-it-all.
- Remember, honesty and sincerity will carry you to your future destination.

Chapter 13
Foster an Environment of Thinkers

The human possibility that is essential for the growth and development of your employees is the ability to think independently. As a leader, you need to know how to help your employees see and think differently, to step outside the box and seek new knowledge, which should help with the final outcome on quality care delivery and a creative working environment.

How can you help promote thinking? By helping in the creation of an environment that fosters it. There is a possibility for the individual to think independently when the environment is good and right for self-evaluation and awareness. This awareness can allow the individual to tap into his or her resources and hidden talents for the sake. Employees are always willing to contribute when they know that there is value in what is being done, and the value is appreciated by the organization.

When talking about organization and how growth is made possible, Jack Welch alluded in his book on winning titled "winning" that winning should be for everybody it should not be for the organization alone. When your environment is good, when it's encouraging and inviting, employees are able to think logically and meaningfully. They are able to take the extra steps that are necessary for the growth and development. The benefits of a better working environment outweigh its disadvantages. An encouraging working environment promotes productivity, enhances performance, and sustains good quality outcomes.

When people are able to think independently, they are able to help the organization achieve its objectives and goals. They are able to help the organization meet its wants and needs. This in turn helps employees to meet their own needs, their own growth, and life expectations. The goal of any organization and its leadership is to build an organization where people can come and achieve their own life goals and professional goals and objectives. Wining should be for all, and each employee should be able to win with the organization. As Jack said, they should be able to provide for their own families and achieve their lifelong American dream. Your role as a leader should always be on how to assist employees to achieve their objectives.

Care delivery has changed due to improved technology and advancement of clinical practices. The changes that have occurred to health care delivery have brought not only changes to relationships but to working environments. Successful organizations must develop a better mechanism for recruiting and retaining good and knowledgeable workers. Promoting a caring culture will depend on their leaders' behaviors. Albrecht has drawn on his long-term experiences in human relations and organizational development to challenge organizational leaders to institute a nurturing behavioral culture within their organizations. The author defines social intelligence (SI) as "the ability to get along well with others and to get them to cooperate with you." These abilities are the most important ingredients in our efforts to develop successful relationships with each other. It was this view from Albrecht that affected my initial beliefs about leaders, management, and the service delivery. Good service delivery will come from a solid organization's cultural values and norms. Values come from the leaders' moral values and behaviors, as demonstrated in his daily practices. If this is the case, we can then ask ourselves whether better management and good service delivery are a function of the social skills of those people delivering or managing the industry.

This book is about the social skills that are important for you to have as a health care worker or leader that can help promote human thinking and creativity. According to Rakich et al. (1992), any leader who wants to be seen as an effective and influential manager should be proficient in these highly significant and relevant areas:

- human relations
- conceptual thinking
- technical skills

Your personal management style will help create a dominant culture of performance, and will pave the way to a competitive advantage for your organization. As a leader, you must recognize the importance of respect, involvement, communication, and the impact of positive interdependency on group synergy and individual performance. As a manager, you must understand that the old hierarchical, top-to-bottom approach will not help you to succeed in a new and changing work environment. It's your ability to change to a new form of management style—one that is open, organic, and most importantly, intellectually challenging—that will help you to be a successful manager.

Instituting a bottom-up approach will help build trust, which is crucial to creating a better working environment.

The open approach of the leader has been shown to produce high associate engagement, which leads to better associate participation and involvement. The approach can also lead to a better relationship between you and your followers, a strong corporate culture, better employee satisfaction and good customer service and retention. The old general belief is that motivation to perform is a function of three ingredients: the leader, the follower, and the situation. For any appropriate leadership style, there is a probability that the follower has the greatest potential to perform and produce the desired outputs.

To move from a stagnant organization to a productive organization, the leaders must know how to work with others for the sake of the organization. Bringing everybody together helps them to understand the values and potentials that each is bringing to the organization. Thinking employee always look at tomorrow, and examine all the variables before engaging in any behavior. Thinking employees are futuristic; they are goal getters and appreciate efforts of all instead of one.

To be a successful leader in today's working environment, he or she must believe in the collective efforts of all people and be ready to create and foster a culture wherein people have a tremendous opportunity to feel heard, valued, and respected for their contributions. When all these attributes begin to happen, people will begin to see the leader as someone that recognizes values in diversity, and see diversity as a measure of unity, as well as a process of bringing out the best from people.

Working together as a body should be the centerpiece of organizational decision-making and a means of building a better community. When everybody feels the connectedness of working together as a unified body, things become more integrated with common objectives and intentions. The result of this connectedness is that body, soul, and mind start coming together for the sake of the organization, instead of being all over the place. When employees begin to see themselves as one, they are able to think together, reason together, and grow together, which is good for the organization.

To promote thinkers in the organization, the environment must be

1. a trusted working environment;
2. an environment that believes in its people;
3. an environment where working together as a team is a norm that is cherished all and not just few;
4. an environment that seeks potential talent and helps

develop it for the sake the organization; and
5. an environment that appreciates changes and permits an internal structure that meaningful and useful for all, an environment where communication is a t way street, and nobody is at a higher status than anyone else.

Conclusion

Effective leaders are not born, they're made. And they are not made once; they're made over and over again. The leadership styles you may have used at one organization are not likely to be beneficial at another. In the same vein, if you are promoted or transferred to another department within the same organization, you may be required to also change your leadership style.

If your goal is to be an effective manager no matter what environment you're in, then the information you have just read in this book, including the professional examples of what to do and not do and the summarizing points to remember at the end of each chapter should become part of who you are as a leader. Some of the information in this book, specifically those things that are about you as a leader, can be implemented as soon as you complete reading this conclusion. Others, those things that involve changing organizational culture, for example, can take time and investment from others. But if you follow the roadmap given to you in this book, you will be on your way to cultivating leadership from within yourself, your employees, and your organization. Thank you for allowing me to help you on your journey!

Bibliography

Amabile, Teresa. "How to Kill Creativity." *Harvard Business Review* 76, (1997): 77–8.

Atkinson, Philip. "How to Implement Change Effectively." *Institute of Management Services* (2014). This is what I found

Avolio, BJ and WL Gardener. "Authentic Leadership Development: Getting to the Root of Positive Forms of Leadership." *Leadership Quarterly* no. 16, (2005): 315–38.

Barbuto, JE Jr. "Motivation and Transactional, Charismatic, and Transformational Leadership: A Test of Antecedents." *Journal of Leadership and Organizational Studies* 11, no. 4, (2005): 26–40.

Bass, BM. "Does the Transactional-Transformational Leadership Paradigm Transcend Organizational and National Boundaries?" *American Psychologist* 52, (1997): 130–9.

Brown, ME, LK Trevino, and DA Harrison. "Ethical Leadership: Asocial Learning Perspective for Construct Development and Testing." *Organizational Behavior and Human Decision Processes* 97, (2005): 117–34.

Colquitt, JA, RA Noe, and CL Jackson. "Justice in Teams: Antecedents and Consequences of Procedural Justice Climate." *Personnel Psychology* 55, (2002): 83–109.

Collins, J. *Good to Great: Why Some Companies Make the Leap ... and Others Don't.* New York: Harper Business, 2005.

Carter, D and T Baghurst. (2014). "The Influence of Servant Leadership on Restaurant Employee Engagement." *Journal of Business Ethics* 124, (2014): 453–64.

Dunn, Rose and Theo Haimann. *Health Care Management,* 3rd ed. Chicago: Health Administration Press, 2015.

Ebrahimi Mehrabani, S and Azmi Mohamad Noor. "New Approach to Leadership Skills Development (Developing a Model and Measure)," *Journal of Management Development.* Vol. 34, no 7 (2015),33.

Erikson, P. "Effective Communication." *Communication World* no. 11 (1992).

Ferdman, BM, A Avigdor, D Braun, et al. "Collective Experience of Inclusion, Diversity, and Performance in Work Groups." *RAM. Revista de Administracao Mackenzie* no. 11, (2010): 6–26.

Fiedler et al. (2012). Fiedler's Contingency Theory: Practical Application of the Least Preferred Coworker (LPC) Scale. *The IUP Journal of Organizational Behavior, Vol. X, No. 4, October 2011, pp. 7-26*

Bass and Riggio's (2006) Transformational Leadership Model as a Means of Leader-Renewal at the Napa Community Seventh-day Adventist Church" (2011). Project Documents. Paper 53.

Hartnell, C, A. Kinicki, J. Angelo, and Lisa Schurer Lambert et al. "Do Similarities or Differences between CEO Leadership and organizational culture Have a More Positive Effect on Firm Performance? A Test of Competing Predictions" *Journal of Applied Psychology,* Vol 101, no. 6 (Jun 2016), 846–61.

Jack Welch (with Suzy Welch) (2013). "Winning". Gardner Books NY

Perez, Joseph Warren L. (2014) *Impact of nurse Managers' Leadership styles on staff Nurses' Intent to Turnover,* Gardner-Webb University (Published by this university)

Maxwell, J. *The 15 Invaluable Laws of Growth: Live Them and Reach Your Potential.* Boston: Hachette, 2012.

Martin, Michael G. F. "The Limits of Self-Awareness". *Philosophical Studies,* 120 nos. 1–3 (2004), 37–89.

Philips, DT. *Martin Luther King, Jr. on Leadership: Inspiration and Wisdom for Challenging Times.* New York: Business Plus, 2000.

Pless, N and T. Maak. "Building an Inclusive Diversity Culture: Principles, Processes, and Practices." *Journal of Business Ethics* 54, (2004): 129-147.

Greenleaf, RK. (1970). "The Servant as a Leader". Greenleaf Center. GA (this is a book Rakich, JS, et al. *Managing Health Services Organizations.* Baltimore, MD: Health Professions Press, Inc., 1992.

Senge, P. *The Fifth Discipline: The Art and Practice of the Learning Organization.* New York: Doubleday-Currency:, 1990.

Stonehouse, David. "Resistance to Change: the Organization Dimension." *British Journal of Health Care Assistant* 7, no. 3 (2013): 150–1.

Thornton, B, Gary Peltier, and George Perreault. "Systems Thinking: A Skill to Improve Student Achievement." *The Clearing House* 77, no. 5 (May–Jun 2004): 222–7.

Trevino, LK et al. "Moral Person and Moral Manager: How Executives Develop a Reputation for Ethical Leadership." *California Management Review* 42, (2000): 128–42.

Vakola, M and Ioannis Nikolaou. "Attitudes toward Organizational Change: What Is the Role of Employees' Stress and Commitment?" *Employee Relations* 27, no. 2, (2005): 160–74.

Wu, Tsung-Yu, Changya Hu, and Ding-Yu Jiang. "Is Subordinate's Loyalty a Precondition of Supervisor's Benevolent

Leadership? The Moderating Effects of Supervisor's Altruistic Personality and Perceived Organizational Support." *Asian Journal of Social Psychology* 15, (2012): 145–55.

End Notes

[1] Chad Hartnell, A. Kinicki, et al. "Do Similarities or Differences between CEO Leadership and Organizational Culture Have a More Positive Effect on Firm Performance? A Test of Competing Predictions," *Journal of Applied Psychology*, Vol 101(6), Jun 2016.

[2] Shadi Ebrahimi Mehrabani and Azmi Mohamad. "New Approach to Leadership Skills Development (Developing a Model and Measure)," *Journal of Management Development*, Vol. 34 (7), 2015.

www.ingramcontent.com/pod-product-compliance
Lightning Source LLC
LaVergne TN
LVHW021048100526
838202LV00079B/4832